Resumes & Cover Letters

STEVEN PROVENZANO

DEARBORN™
A **Kaplan Professional** Company

This publication is designed to provide accurate and authoritative information in regard to the subject matter covered. It is sold with the understanding that the publisher is not engaged in rendering legal, accounting, or other professional service. If legal advice or other expert assistance is required, the services of a competent professional person should be sought.

Associate Publisher: Cynthia A. Zigmund
Senior Managing Editor: Jack Kiburz
Interior Design: Lucy Jenkins
Cover Design: Design Alliance, Inc.
Typesetting: Elizabeth Pitts

Published by Dearborn, a Kaplan Professional Company

Printed in the United States of America

01 02 10 9 8 7

Library of Congress Cataloging-in-Publication Data

Provenzano, Steven.
    Top secret resumes and cover letters / by Steven Provenzano.
      p. cm.
    Includes index.
    ISBN 0-7931-1359-8 (paper
    1. Résumés (Employment)   2. Cover letters. I. Title.
    808'06665—dc20   95-16477
                                                       CIP

Contents

Work Force • Basic versus Effective Statements • Power/
Action Words

Preface

Congratulations for picking up this book. You've just done more to improve your resume—and your career outlook—than most people ever will.

That's because there are still people who downplay the importance of resumes, usually because theirs has never helped them get an interview. They say to me: "I'll talk about myself at the interview." But there's the catch: you may not get the interview if your resume doesn't *market your abilities* with precision and impact.

After writing more than 4,000 resumes in my career with leading resume firms including my own, and more than a year in corporate recruiting, I can tell you the most important fact of job-hunting: the best person doesn't always get the interview. Rather, it's the person who presents himself or herself in the most clear, concise and professional manner.

This guide will show you how to write a high-impact, *self-marketing tool* that does justice to you and your hard-earned skills. Whether you're a seasoned executive or straight out of school, there's an average and an excellent way to present yourself on paper. It's time to transform your resume from a listing of your past (no matter how well listed) to a future-oriented document that can greatly increase your income and job satisfaction.

This book was created and refined with direct feedback from our resume clients and through conversations with hiring authorities. The information and samples will bring you up-to-date on what employers want to see in a resume. It is time to use this knowledge to expand your career.

By the way, this is the first book to offer a free resume analysis and consultation by the author or his staff. See page 217 for specific directions on how to take advantage of valuable assistance.

CHAPTER 1

The Secrets of Creating an Effective Resume

A WORLD OF PERMANENT CHANGE

It is the middle of the '90s and the economy is getting stronger or weaker, depending on whom you believe. Unemployment is down and newspapers are full of "jobs." Yet people seem to be searching for more rewarding, higher quality positions.

The strength of our economy is due in large part to corporate downsizing. Large companies are cutting staff and expect more output from fewer personnel. Too many high-quality professionals and executives are on the street or fear they might be soon. But smaller companies are cropping up everywhere and can provide excellent opportunities for well-trained, experienced personnel.

This is why it is so essential that your resume sell your skills and abilities.

Competition for good, well-paying jobs is fierce, and as companies get leaner and meaner, an equally lean and mean resume is essential to your job search. A resume is your life, your career on paper, and often the first impression employers will have of your skills, experience and professional standards.

The Big Picture

Even if you're a new college graduate, there is so much more you can do with your resume than list your name, classes and part-time jobs. Although most of my resume clients are professionals and executives, I recently wrote a resume for a new college graduate who sent 20 resumes, received four interviews and four job offers, and has since found a great job. This is an excellent response, but not impossible when using the writing techniques in this book. (That resume can be found on page 96.)

The resumes and cover letters in this book were written by me for my clients. Names of job hunters and companies have been changed, of course, and I encourage you to scan as many samples as possible for key words and phrases to use in your resume.

I really can't stress this enough! Please take the time to use the samples and tips in this book because it can make the difference between getting a job next week or three months from now, or between a starting salary of $40,000 or $48,000. I've seen this happen many times, and there are several reasons why.

BASIC VERSUS EFFECTIVE RESUMES

Many people think writing a resume is simple. They write brief descriptions of their work history and education, have it typeset—or typed and photocopied—and hope for the best. The results are usually not very good. They probably don't know what they're up against. A typical one-inch advertisement in the Sunday paper can draw hundreds of resumes, and research tells us that most of these have only a few seconds to grab the reader's attention and get him or her to read the entire resume, let alone call you in for a personal interview.

When people walk into my office and ask me to write a "simple" or "basic" resume, I tell them there's no such thing. There are only resumes that are more or less effective, depending on how well they are written and used.

Writing a great resume becomes easier when you think of it as a discovery process. This is your chance to analyze your knowledge and accomplishments in your chosen field and decide what direction your career should take. This process helps prepare you for interview questions and can actually create new career choices, because you may see your experience as being applicable to new positions or even whole new industries.

Resumes are here to stay as a necessary part of the business world. A resume can lead to more and better interviews, or it can cost you job opportunities. The resume game is a numbers game, and the only way to win is to outwrite your competitors. Don't let someone less qualified than you get *your* interview just because he or she has a better resume!

Let's Get Real

Contrary to books that claim otherwise, a resume cannot get you a job; only you can do that. But a resume certainly can help you get decent interviews. It can also prevent you from getting a job, when it's ineffective and employers ruthlessly "weed you out" because of it. Believe me, this happens every day. Once you get some on-target interviews, the resume becomes secondary and you get the chance to sell your qualifications personally.

I encourage you to respond to advertisements as part of your job search. But keep in mind that many of the best positions are never advertised and are filled through personal networking or referrals.

☞ *Tipster . . .*

Personal networking is really the best way to get a job. You should talk with former coworkers and clients, friends and family members, and you should call target companies.

Mailing out a resume isn't the only way to get an interview.

Market studies show that 60 to 80 percent of professionals get their jobs through informed referrals, about 15 percent are filled through search firms, 10 percent through mass mailings and only about 5 percent through published advertisements. Still, an excellent resume is essential for all these methods and you should always be prepared: keep five or six resumes in the back seat of your car in a 9 × 12 envelope; you never know when you'll need one.

Job listings in the newspaper may be helpful, but you may find that many of them pay less than what you're making now, or that you are overqualified or underqualified for them. See Chapter 10, "Using Your Resume Effectively," for alternative uses of resumes.

WHAT IS A TOP SECRET RESUME?

This book is called *Top Secret Resumes & Cover Letters* because it contains *improved and refined* writing and format secrets used by many (though certainly not all) professional resume writers nationwide.

After working for some of the nation's largest resume companies, perhaps the most valuable secret I could tell you is that while there are many excellent writers in our industry, there are some who aren't quite as good as they claim to be. Mom-and-pop shops open and close on a regular basis, and it seems everyone with a computer and time to spare is an "expert" on resumes. It's important to understand that quality of work can vary widely, just as it does in any business.

Having said this, I would like to encourage you to shop the professional resume services in your area after reading this book, or if you find you're too busy to deal with the writing and printing chores. Check the phone book for reputable services in your area or contact our offices directly with the phone and fax numbers listed in this book. Getting an experienced writer to proofread, edit or assist with your resume can be extremely valuable.

GETTING HELP FROM A RESUME SERVICE

Be sure the writer you select is not merely a typist, a printer, or just someone who owns a computer. He or she should have written at least 1,000 resumes and should have one, preferably two years of full-time experience. Remember that resume professionals don't do this as a sideline. The person should have a college degree or extensive training in journalism, writing or English.

Expect to pay $90 to $175 for *total composition* of a one-page resume, including a personal interview/analysis of your skills, with or without a cover letter. Two-page resumes can run between $185 and $295. All writing or editing should include at least ten laser prints (not photocopies) on linen or laid paper. Be sure the writing techniques are at least similar to those in this book. Better yet: use this book to write the best resume you can, then call our office or one in your area and pay only for laser printing or editing, which runs between $40 and $75.

Many services, including our own, can write, customize and mail cover letters. This can be a valuable time-saving measure and your envelope can also be addressed and personalized. We can also target your resume to employment services and headhunters by geographic location or industry.

Resume Style and Philosophy

The resumes in this book not only have impact and raw data; they also have a degree of style and grace, things you must keep in mind when writing your self-marketing tool. Of course, no resume guide can tell you the exact wording that'll work best for you, but these resumes demonstrate techniques I've used successfully for thousands of clients in almost every field. They are the result of direct feedback from my clients and from employers and were refined through trial and error. Not every profession is represented, but I've included a cross-section of the most common positions.

It is best to read this entire guide before sitting down to write, but you may also skip ahead to the resume examples for words and phrases that best suit your needs. If you still need help writing about yourself, by all means call us or check your library for resume samples related to your individual profession if they're not included here. Because many resume guides offer conflicting advice or less effective/outdated formats, look for language related to the job you're seeking and use the formats and writing techniques presented here.

A list of active verbs is included for use in both the Experience (Summary) and Employment sections, discussed later. As for adjectives, be sure to use them sparingly. When managers or personnel representatives come across vast wastelands of gobbledygook, they may just scan every job title you've had and look for one that vaguely matches their needs. If one doesn't catch their eye, then it's on to the next one in the stack and all that expensive paper and typesetting was for naught. Remember, it is always *content* that matters most. Paper, typeface and format are important, but they run second place to content in the reader's mind.

As long as you've purchased this book, I encourage you to *Go ahead and make a mess of it.*

Feel free to make notes in the margins and circle phrases and instructions that apply specifically to your situation. The more you mark up this book, the more involved you're getting in the writing process and the better your resume will be.

Now on to a better future . . .

CHAPTER 2

Market Your Abilities

The most important point to keep in mind when writing your resume is: Put yourself in the employer's position. Always remember the basic question that runs through the mind of every employer who picks up your resume:

Just what can *you* do for me?

If I'm an employer with hundreds of resumes sitting on my desk, why should I call you? Because you think you have a great work history? Because of the paper color you picked for your resume? This harks back to the typical Chronological (job description) style resume that was probably used by the first cave dwellers seeking positions as shaman or lead tiger hunter.

☞ *Tipster...*

> As a busy executive or corporate recruiter, I don't have all day to read every little aspect about what you think is a great work history. I mostly want to know *what you can do for me*, in the here and now, for my particular operation. But all you're telling me with a Chronological resume is *what you've done for someone else.*

Of course, your work history and education are very important to your resume and must be included when applicable. Employers need to know where you worked and/or went to school, and these items should be used to your best advantage.

But the "Tipster" above is really the key point of this book, and to truly understand it means taking a giant leap forward in getting more interviews with your resume. This paragraph sounds so simple; yet how many resumes have a Summary or Profile section (also called the Experience section) that tells the reader in clear, no-nonsense language what skills and abilities the applicant can bring to a company? *Very few!*

So come out and tell employers what you can do for them, and do it with style. Hit them over the head with your true, quantifiable, applicable skills and abilities that you've *extracted* from your work history, education, volunteer work or whatever. This is what employers want to know, and must be told, as soon as they pick up your resume.

Write your resume on the premise that employers are lazy and don't want to think. Reading stacks of resumes can quickly become a tedious, dreaded task. Never trust an employer to read your entire resume. Because most resumes get so little time to impress a reader, tell them in no uncertain terms:

1. *In the Experience section:* The most applicable skills and abilities you can bring to a company that can help you learn and/or execute the position better than anyone else
2. *In the Employment or Career Background section (or Education or Highlights if you really have* no *work history at all):* Where you applied or learned those skills and what they've achieved for previous or current employers, volunteer groups, your family or anyone else

BRAIN SURGERY—GETTING INTO THE MIND OF AN EMPLOYER

Here's where you take the next giant leap in resume writing: get into the mind of the employer. Another way of saying this is: *Do the thinking for the employer.* Employers don't want to think about your past; they want to interview decent candidates and get someone hired, usually ASAP.

Market the skills and abilities you wish to use most *and which you think employers want to see.* Determine this through research of the company, a job listing, advertisement, industry knowledge and so on. This is delivered right near the top in the Experience section. It is then reinforced, qualified and proven by what those same talents have produced for previous employers.

☞ *Tipster . . .*

Your new resume must be future oriented, so always keep this distinction in mind: there are skills you can bring to your new employer and duties you would like to perform (Experience section) *and then* there are those duties and achievements that have taken place at previous jobs or in school (Employment and/or Education section). Isolate and market your skills apart from where they were performed; *then* back them up with company/school names, dates and so on.

Employers may wonder: Does this person know how to utilize (or program) the computer systems my company uses? Can he or she use the latest marketing databases and help increase sales? Can this applicant interpret the federal government's recent changes in statutes regarding environmental issues? Put yourself in the employer's place and these questions get much easier to ask—and to answer.

If you're a new college graduate, draw on any part-time work experiences, no matter how irrelevant they may seem (e.g., fast-food places or clothing stores). Otherwise, set aside your lack of job experience and think about the skills you actually learned in school and sell them on top: the ability to plan and conduct presentations, research and write detailed reports, or utilize certain software (and to what extent). See Chapter 5, "Outlines for the Major Professions." Everyone from first-time job seekers to housewives returning to the work force to veterans and established professionals can make use of this concept to get a better position.

☞ *Tipster . . .*

> **Do what most people fail to do in their resume: market all your *applicable* skills developed throughout your life experience, regardless of *where* or *why* they were performed, then qualify them under an employment or education section when possible.**

This must be done just right, or it may backfire: write about your tangible skills and forget the fluff about being "a hands-on professional with a strong desire to excel in a challenging environment" (blah, blah, blah).

Truth and substance are what employers really want and must comprehend before they call you in for an interview. It's up to you to spell all this out in your resume, and the way you do tells the reader as much about who you are as what you want from your career.

This point was driven home recently when I spoke with two top personnel executives at Motorola's national headquarters in Schaumburg, Illinois.

TWO CORPORATE RECRUITERS SPEAK OUT

Rodney Gee is Manager of Staffing and Billy Dexter is Manager of University Relations for the Land Mobile Products Sector, one of six sectors at Motorola Corporation. Talk about swamped—these guys get up to *600* resumes per week from executives, professionals and new graduates.

"We don't have much time to look at a resume, so it must have structure and consistency," said Dexter. "If a resume is too broad, we'll pass it over. Tell us about special projects, skill sets, computer languages, leadership activities, people- or team-leading skills and things outside the classroom. If I have to search through a resume for these items, I probably won't read it."

Your Experience section gives you control over your resume and lets you focus on the key points Dexter and Gee are looking for. If you do use an Objective, both recruiters said it shouldn't be "rosy" and "must quickly define what the applicant is looking for in one or two sentences."

Careful Omission

What you leave out of your resume is just as important as what you leave in. It's O.K. to break some rules of grammar in the interest of brevity, but limit this to sentences that take *I, we, he, she* and other pronouns for granted. Omit these words altogether. Use the abbreviated third-person voice demonstrated in the Experience sections throughout this book. It is succinct, direct and helps you get straight to your qualifications and *MARKET* them.

Two Qualifying Points

When space is tight or if you really must have all your qualifications on one page, you can sacrifice or reduce the Experience section in favor of applicable work experience. However, don't be afraid of a two-page resume. They are much more acceptable in these days of increased staff turnover. Besides, a two-page resume lets you use more white space and larger type, two excellent ways to increase the readability of your document. More on this later in Chapter 6.

The Experience section may be omitted for physicians, attorneys or high-level executives in finance where many employers still like to see conservative, Chronological listings of jobs and accomplishments. Teachers and college professors may also omit the Experience section when it pushes you into a second page.

SMASHING SOME MAJOR MYTHS

Always keep in mind that people get jobs, not resumes. It's up to you to get the job through research, effective written and oral correspondence, and professional interviewing. And remember, a resume style that works for one person may not work for you. An effective job search often hinges on a combination of your individual talents, your industry and the job market at any given time. I've had customers walk in with badly written resumes they claim have gotten them interviews. That's because their skills were in demand at a certain place and time and they were such a good match for the position (perhaps the applicant worked for a key competitor or was a well-known customer or business associate) that the employer didn't care so much about resume content.

However, a perfect resume is essential for *the rest of us* competing for a dearth of decent jobs in a tough economy. That is why there's really no "best" resume format or writing technique; only those that seem to work more often than others or are tailored for certain situations. Just because a resume style or format seemed to attract interviews for your brother's friend's wife does not mean it will work for you.

MOST POPULAR FORMATS

The *format* for most samples in this book is the *Combination* format. It is conservative, clean, direct and works best for about 90 percent of our resume clients. Those seeking positions in advertising, marketing, desktop publishing or other creative fields are encouraged to experiment with graphics, lines or other methods to show off their creativity.

The Combination format uses the best aspects of a Functional resume (achievements/abilities only, followed by job/company titles and no job descriptions) at the top, combined with a Chronological resume (job & school descriptions and no summary) near the end.

The Combination format (which usually includes Experience, Employment and Education sections, with bullets), is used by many resume companies, but the actual wording varies widely. Specific wordings and formats have been refined for this book.

CHAPTER 3

Getting Started:
The Raw Materials

ASSESSING YOUR SKILLS AND ABILITIES

Before you can write anything about your background, you need to start answering every employer's question: "What can you do for me?"

The *personal assessment sheet* and various worksheets included in this chapter will help you organize your thoughts. To complete your personal assessment, stand back and take a long look at your total career background related to the position you're seeking. (For new college graduates, this means getting an idea of how the things you've learned relate to the position you're seeking.) Make notes about your marketable skills and abilities, *whether or not you've used them on the job. Extract* your best skills from your jobs, education or *anywhere* and market them in your Experience section.

The Job Duties and Accomplishments listing should represent a general, overall summary of your achievements for previous employers, such as the ability to meet or exceed sales quotas (by what percentage?), success in developing new product designs or business systems and so on. When writing your resume, you'll use only the best of these.

Notice we're really talking about overall *ability* here, not just work history or education, and there is a difference. A college graduate may have many abilities (developed through courses, special projects, internships, volunteer/organizational work, etc.) and very little work history. The best way that person can get his or her first "real" job is to market all of his or her ability. Think of the *type* of work you've done for college projects, charitable organizations or special groups: "report preparation and analysis; data compilation and review; plan and conduct written and oral presentations in a professional manner," etc. This, combined with your education and knowledge of the field, will help project you as a viable candidate for the position.

No matter who you are or how great you can write, a *truly* professional writer can probably improve your resume.

Now you must become your own professional writer. Because I can't sit across from you and ask questions about your experience and education, you must do it yourself. This requires honesty and objectivity. Are you really proficient at *everything* you do? Of course not. On the other hand, don't take any of your applicable experience for granted. It can be fatal to assume employers already know what you can do simply because they are already in that particular business.

Imagine yourself already in the position. Think about how your qualifications can be shaped into phrases a job incumbent would appreciate. If you're not sure exactly what field interests you, don't worry. Check the examples indexed under *General Employment* and just start writing. Write down everything you think of first, then narrow it down and make a short list of those items you feel are most applicable to the desired position. Make constant comparisons with the resume examples.

ITEMS YOU SHOULD INCLUDE IN YOUR RESUME

For help in nailing down these essential items, be sure to use the worksheets in Figures 3.1 and 3.2.

1. *Your name, address and phone number.* Some people forget to include their phone number on their resume. As a recruiter with two corporations, I received resumes without phone numbers and, of course, those applicants didn't get far with us.

2. *Company names and dates.* Unless you've had four or five jobs shorter than one year and are writing a functional resume, include company names and branches or divisions if that helps describe your responsibilities. Also include the towns/cities and states, using postal abbreviations (e.g., IL) Dates are preferred: use months as well as years, or omit months if it helps you leave out jobs or cover your tracks, but be consistent!

3. *Job titles.* You should modify your job titles when needed for clarity and to give an identification that can be understood by as many employers as possible. For instance: Level Four Packer/Shipper can be written as Shipper/Packer and Assistant Collections Representative as Collections Representative.

4. *Job responsibilities.* Most employers must review your work history before considering you. Include part-time employment when the experience applies to the position desired. You may also include part-time jobs or volunteer work that shows initiative, self-motivation, leadership or organizational/communication skills.

5. *Licenses and certifications.* You should include licenses for Insurance and Real Estate sales, and of course, other applicable credentials such as

CPA. Include civil service or government grades and classifications when appropriate for the type of job you are seeking.

6. *Education.* List the highest level reached first and avoid listing high school education if you have a college degree. If you've recently left school with no hands-on or applicable work experience, describe your education right after your Experience section.

   Education becomes less important as your hands-on work experience grows. Place it just below Employment if you have at least one year of applicable work history. You may include college attendance and course completions even if you did not earn a degree. Always ask yourself: is this applicable to my present career goal? Include additional professional training, especially if it was sponsored by an employer: it shows the company had confidence in your ability to learn and succeed. List which firms sponsored the seminars or college courses. Also include whether you *self-funded* more than 80 percent of college costs.

7. *Patents and publications.* Definitely list articles published in magazines, trade journals and newspapers. You should also list patents on product designs or production techniques and summarize the technical knowledge in your Experience/Profile section.

8. *Professional groups.* Listing affiliations or memberships with professional groups shows you have an active interest in industry developments. It may also show that you share ideas with other professionals in your field. These affiliations can prove very valuable in your job search when you get to personal networking, discussed in Chapter 10.

9. *Languages.* You can mention your languages in a short line at the end of your Experience section and list your level of proficiency: "Speak conversational Spanish," "Fluent in French," "Read and Write Italian," "Familiar with Russian." Otherwise, list them at or near the bottom in a Personal section.

ITEMS YOU SHOULD OMIT FROM YOUR RESUME

In the resume examples that follow, you will see no mention of the following items:

1. *The word* Resume *at the top of the page or* References Available Upon Request *at the end.* If your resume cannot be easily identified as such, something needs rewriting. For references, write three to six names, titles and phone numbers of previous supervisors, if you are sure they will give you a positive reference. Have these printed on the same quality and color of paper as your resume. Bring this page along with your resume to complete the job application. The personnel representative or hiring manager will probably call your last two or three employers and try to speak directly with your former supervisors if the company is serious about hiring you. Usually someone will check with

you before contacting your current employer, but if you are concerned about confidentiality, mention this at the interview.

2. *Reasons for leaving a job.* If a potential employer wants to know why or how you left a job, they can call you and ask. This gives them a reason to call you and gives you the chance to further discuss how you can benefit them. You should expect to be asked about reasons for leaving other positions, so prepare yourself prior to the interview. If your last few jobs were unusually short and there are genuinely good reasons for leaving, such as relocation or major company cutbacks due to industry trends, include a one-line explanation at the end of your job responsibilities. This is very rare and is suggested only if your employment history is spotty and you're getting no response from the first 40 or 50 resumes mailed.

3. *Salary requirements/history.* If an employer asks for this information in an advertisement or job posting, then include it with your resume, but on a separate Salary History sheet and never on the resume. If salary requirements are requested, you can give them a *salary range* in your cover letter, such as ". . . seeking a position in the upper 40s per year; however, this is negotiable depending on the position, benefits and the potential for greater income." At one of my resume seminars, an audience member *did not* include his salary history and received an interview, even though the advertisement read "resumes without salary history will not be considered." If salary information is not requested, don't offer it. You could be passed over for a position simply because you're seen as overpriced or underpriced. Try to concentrate on the interview first and getting an employer interested in you; then negotiate compensation.

4. *Religious or political organizations.* All of us have our prejudices and this information can have a better chance of working against you than for you. Remember to put business considerations first. Do these associations have anything to do with the position you're seeking? Like anything else, if it won't actually help you get in the door, leave it out. You can make an exception to this rule if you have confusing, little, or no work history, but good experience with churches, synagogues, or social events and groups, such as Rotary Clubs or the Kiwanis. Business fraternities and associations are O.K. to list. Develop and include this experience on your resume by extracting your best communication, organizational and/or leadership skills used with these groups and paraphrasing them in your Experience section: "Organize groups and community events"; "familiar with advertising, fund-raising and strategic planning."

5. *Negative information.* To many employers, resume reading is a process of elimination and you must not give the reader any reason to take you out of the running. Never mention lawsuits, a bad experience with a

former boss, or other information that could be seen as negatively affecting your performance on the job.

☞ *Tipster . . .*

A resume is all of your positives and none of your negatives. Employers know this as well as you do and the best ones know how to read between the lines. When they do, there must always be truth and substance to your writing. Avoid cliche phrases like "a seasoned professional," "a motivated self-starter" or "displays warmth and affection for all people." Believe it or not, people have used all these phrases on resumes! Omit items if you must or can, but NEVER LIE on your resume. A lie may catch up with you.

OPTIONAL INFORMATION

1. *Personal or interests section.* If you really need to fill room at the bottom of the page, include two to three lines outlining your interests in sports and/or exercise. Golf and racquet sports are great for executives. List team sports such as college or park district basketball or baseball, especially if you were team captain, showing leadership. Adding "avid reader and chess player" demonstrates reading and analytical skills and is recommended. Avoid items that have no connection to tackling the job, such as "enjoy basket weaving, crocheting and cooking."

2. *Age and marital status.* Legally, these two items should have no bearing on whether you're considered for a position, but often that's not the case. Listing your age (birthday) can label you as too young or too old no matter what your age. Leave it out all together. Omit marital status, unless you are sure this will demonstrate a certain stability and improve your chances of getting an interview for positions such as part of a husband/wife franchise team or as marriage counselor.

3. *Military service.* You should include positive military service, especially when seeking a position with a firm involved in defense contracting, which hires former military personnel. Include your highest rank attained, supervisory experience and applicable training. For technical positions, include systems and equipment operated, repaired or maintained. If your only applicable work experience was in the military, then of course this must be developed like any other job. In this case, label the section EMPLOYMENT rather than MILITARY.

4. *Disabilities.* Under the Americans with Disabilities Act, companies with 15 or more employees are not allowed to ask about disabilities on applications. I view this as a truly personal choice: omit this information if you think it can harm your interview prospects, but if you feel better about being up front with employers, mention it in one or two short sentences under a Personal section at the bottom.

FIGURE 3.1 Personal Assessment

Skills and Abilities	Duties and Accomplishments
Skill Group:	At most recent company:
(Summarize specific industry knowledge, training, abilities or actual experience: acctg. skills, sales, mgmt., customer service, etc.)	(If just out of college, include specific college classes, projects, internships, volunteer groups, etc., where skills were learned or applied.)
Skill Group:	At company #2:
(Expand on the above skill group: payroll or AP/AR, sales presentations/product knowledge, staff training/ supervision and so on.)	
Skill Group:	At company #3:
(Expand even further on all of the above, or summarize less specific attributes: communication, organizational and/or analytical.)	
Skill Group:	At company #4:
(Use these items for 4th or 5th bullet points, used primarily for two-page resumes. See the examples and continue to expand on marketable skills & abilities.)	

FIGURE 3.2 Worksheets

First Name _____ Middle Initial _____

Last Name _____

Street _____ City _____ State _____ Zip _____

Home Ph. with Area Code _____ / _____

Fax or Car Ph. _____ / _____ Work Ph. *if safe to include* _____ / _____

TITLE/OBJECTIVE or INDUSTRY DESIRED: _____

EMPLOYMENT List most recent *or relevant* position first:

From   Company _____

_____ 19____   City/State _____

To   Type of Business or Product/Service _____

_____ 19____   Your Positions/Titles _____

Duties/Responsibilities _____

_____

_____

Supervision or Leadership Functions _____

_____

_____

Major Achievements/Awards _____

_____

_____

From   Company _____

_____ 19____   City/State _____

To   Type of Business or Product/Service _____

_____ 19____   Your Positions/Titles _____

Duties/Responsibilities _____

_____

_____

Supervision or Leadership Functions _____

_____

_____

FIGURE 3.2 Worksheets (Continued)

Major Achievements/Awards _____

_____

_____

From   Company _____

_____ 19____   City/State _____

To   Type of Business or Product/Service _____

_____ 19____   Your Positions/Titles _____

Duties/Responsibilities _____

_____

_____

Supervision or Leadership Functions _____

_____

_____

Major Achievements/Awards _____

_____

_____

EDUCATION Most recent *or relevant* first:

University _____ City/State _____

Degree _____ Year(s) Attended/Graduated:_____

(Note: You may omit graduation/attendance dates in light of your age)

Major _____ Minor _____ GPA (B or higher) _____

Key Courses/Studies _____

_____

_____

Awards and/or Scholarships

_____

_____

Seminars/Special Training _____

_____

_____

Vocational/Trade School _____ City/State _____

Certificate _____ Dates Attended _____

FIGURE 3.2 Worksheets (Continued)

Special Jobs and/or Equipment _____

_____

_____

High School _____ Dates Attended _____

Military Service: _____ Dates Enlisted _____

Honorably Discharged? _____ Rank_____

_____

_____

Professional/Industry Memberships:

Organization Dates _____

Any Offices Held? _____

Responsibilities/Duties _____

Skills Acquired _____

_____

_____

Organization _____ Dates _____

Any Offices Held? _____

Responsibilities/Duties _____

Skills Acquired   _____

_____

_____

Organization _____ Dates _____

Any Offices Held? _____

Responsibilities/Duties _____

Skills Acquired   _____

_____

_____

_____

_____

FIGURE 3.2 Worksheets (Continued)

VOLUNTEER ACTIVITIES and/or Community Service:

Organization _____ Offices or Titles Held _____

City/State _____ Dates _____

Activities in which you were involved and skills utilized:

_____

_____

_____

_____

_____

Organization _____ Offices or Titles Held _____

City/State _____ Dates _____

Activities in which you were involved and skills utilized:

_____

_____

_____

_____

_____

PERSONAL INTERESTS Sports or hobbies, preferably related to your skills/job aptitude:

_____

_____

_____

_____

_____

_____

_____

_____

_____

_____

_____

_____

_____

FIGURE 3.2 Worksheets (Continued)

REFERENCES:

Business:

Name _____ His/Her Job Title _____

Company Name _____ City/State _____

Telephone, Office _____ / _____ Home, if allowed _____ / _____

Name _____ His/Her Job Title _____

Company Name _____ City/State _____

Telephone, Office _____ / _____ Home, if allowed _____ / _____

Name _____ His/Her Job Title _____

Company Name _____ City/State _____

Telephone, Office _____ / _____ Home, if allowed _____ / _____

Personal:

Name _____ His/Her Profession _____

Telephone, Office _____ / _____ Home, if allowed _____ / _____

Name _____ His/Her Profession _____

Telephone, Office _____ / _____ Home, if allowed _____ / _____

Name _____ His/Her Profession _____

Telephone, Office _____ / _____ Home, if allowed _____ / _____

NOTES:

_____

_____

_____

_____

_____

_____

_____

_____

_____

_____

_____

_____

THE MOST POPULAR RESUME FORMATS

Depending on whom you talk to and which books you read on the subject, there are hundreds of ways to write and design your resume. Here are three of the best formats, which can be changed to suit your particular qualifications and career goals. My personal favorite is #3, the Combination format.

1. *Reverse Chronological or Chronological.* These are the two most common types of homemade resumes. The Chronological format consists of job descriptions and education in reverse order (beginning with the most recent). Employers, job titles and dates are listed first; responsibilities and achievements follow. Physicians, attorneys and most senior-level executives with solid work experience may use this rather conservative approach. As you will see in the resume examples, the Employment section must concisely emphasize your most important duties with a company, skills used that apply to your career goals, awards or achievements and specific benefits you brought to the company.

   If your most relevant experience was long ago, don't be afraid to place that at the top, Reverse Chronological format, follow it with descriptions and dates of other positions, in order, and end with your present job. Dates should be tucked away in the right-hand margin. If there are gaps of several months between companies, try using only years. Again, if your current or most recent experience is also the most relevant to your goals, it belongs right on top, as the first item of your Employment section.

2. *Functional.* Be aware that this format is often frowned on by employers, because it doesn't tell them where you've been working and they may think you are hiding something (presumed bad) about your background. It also doesn't place your skills or achievements in *context*, so employers may wonder where and when all of it took place.

   This format is best for emphasizing talents and experience most applicable to the position you're seeking, *regardless of employment background.* I recommend it only if there are major gaps in your work history, or between jobs related to your current Objective. It is useful for homemakers or veterans returning to the work force, those with unsuccessful self-employment experience, or anyone with confusing or little work experience.

3. *Combination Chronological/Functional.* This type of resume gives you the best of both the Chronological and Functional worlds. It has proven to work best for my clients because you can market all the best points of your skills, abilities and experience in the Profile/Experience section, then back it up with your work history. If you omit an Objective, the Experience section can give the reader a good idea of the type of position for which you're best suited. The first paragraph of the Experience section summarizes your years of experience. If it's less than two

years or more than 15, omit the number of years of experience and show that you've developed useful, professional talents that can be of value to the business goals of the target firm.

There's one key point to remember when writing your Experience (or Profile) section; it is not meant to be *job specific*, it is meant to be about *your skills and abilities*, primarily the ones you would like to use in your next position. This section gives you the latitude and control you need over your resume. Without such a summary section, you're essentially sending out a history of your past and hoping the employer can find somewhere to fit you in. You must project yourself as *the* person who can tackle the position you're seeking. A short Experience section creates an air of knowledgeability and respectability. Present yourself as a discriminating professional and you have a much better chance of being perceived as one.

These days, much of the feedback I get from employers is that they're not always looking for someone with a "perfect" background, but rather someone who can:

- Learn the position.
- Communicate well.
- Fit into their corporate environment.
- Help them serve their customers and increase their profits.

The Experience section, recommended for most resumes, helps you pinpoint and convey all of these abilities. It's where you *extract* your best talents, acquired through work, education or whatever, and *market/target* those talents to employers.

ONE OR TWO PAGES?

Just about everyone you ask will tell you that a one-page resume is "best." But ask yourself how this can possibly apply to someone with 10 to 15 years of relevant, diverse experience. Simplicity and impact must work together. Although you should not overwhelm employers with too much data, don't leave them guessing and don't think to yourself, "Oh, they know what I mean" because they usually *don't* unless you tell them. If a concise outline of your current, marketable skills and abilities, reinforced by employment and education, requires two or even three pages to be accurately presented, then use two or three pages. However, unless you have a variety of applicable work experience or a detailed technical background of more than five years, one page will probably suffice.

What's best is what works for you. If you write a concise resume that doesn't fit on one page, don't force it to by omitting important facts or sending out a page crammed with type and little or no white space (discussed in Chapter 6), reducing its readability and eye appeal. On the other hand, if you find yourself with only three or four lines of text on page two, you should find some way of editing or reducing type to end up with a one-page resume.

Weeding 'Em Out

Accuracy and quality of writing is essential. As noted earlier, research tells us that the average advertisement has only a few seconds to grab the reader's interest. For the same reason, brevity and overall appearance are key to a successful resume. If you're not sure how to spell a word, look it up. If you don't know how to type accurately, hire a professional writer or printer. Nothing discourages an employer more than basic spelling or grammar mistakes on a resume. The impression is: "If this person can't even write a decent resume, how could he/she handle this job?" Use ample margins (¾" to 1" on all sides) and plenty of white space throughout the page. This makes your personal advertisement more attractive and reduces reader fatigue while increasing the chance that readers will actually connect with the content of your resume.

CHAPTER 4

The Objective, Experience and Employment Sections

SHOULD YOU USE AN OBJECTIVE OR TITLE?

It seems there will always be a debate on whether or not to use an Objective. You should certainly have some idea about what kind of position you're seeking, even if all you know is that you have great analytical skills and want to be challenged when using them on the job. Having an Objective is highly recommended for those who know exactly what position they want. It shows confidence, self-assurance and stability. On the other hand, if you think summarizing your career goals in one or two sentences is just too narrowing or constricting, then leave it out all together. This is what Vicki Spina suggests in *Getting Hired In The '90s.* "There may be other positions available for which they may call you," she says.

Rather than telling readers *"what you want"* from them, you can give them a focus and sense of direction in the Experience section. The bullet points here are a strong nudge to your readers. The first bullet gives him or her a full overview of your most marketable skills, which in turn gives them an idea of what kind of work you're looking for. It is a great way to catch their interest and get them involved in, and focused on, your abilities.

WRITING THE OBJECTIVE OR TITLE

Use an Objective or Title whenever possible, but don't worry about leaving it off if you feel it could limit your job prospects. Here are some examples of statements for your Objective. The first one is intentionally general and applicable for any nonspecific position:

OBJECTIVE: A position utilizing skills in planning, organization and communications.

The best Objectives are specific, with a job title and focus whenever possible:

OBJECTIVE: A Secretarial position where proven abilities in record keeping, typing, filing and client relations would be of value.

OBJECTIVE: Marketing/Sales Support
A position where profit-building skills would be utilized.

Be more specific if you have a number of years of experience, or if you have no room to list the number of years in an Experience section. This example could be used by a Homemaker returning to the work force and the words *home management* could be replaced with just about any profession or industry:

OBJECTIVE: A position utilizing nine years in home management, including budget planning, record keeping, prioritizing and the training/supervision of minors.

Mentioning "training/supervision of minors" might give the reader a chuckle and spark their attention.

When carefully considered, don't worry about misleading anyone with your Objective. It is a simple, yet high-impact way to introduce your resume, and you then quantify and qualify the statement in the Experience and/or Employment sections. Avoid using the word *challenging*. It's just not necessary and, well, burned-out.

How To Use a TITLE

Another option to an Objective is to simply use a Title on top of your Experience section. This consists of one or two words outlining the general type of work or industry you would like to be involved in. It helps give readers a focus by telling *where you're coming from* rather than what you *want* from their company. Examples of Titles include **SALES/MARKETING; ENGINEERING/PRODUCT DESIGN; ACCOUNTING/FINANCE; PROGRAMMER/ANALYST;** or **STAFF TRAINING/DEVELOPMENT.**

Titles are not labeled as such and are typically centered on top of your Experience section. Your relevant skills and abilities then quickly become apparent in each line of your Experience section.

Titles are a great way to give your resume a direction. They can quickly be changed on a master copy and take up very little space. They help you avoid those long, chatty Objectives that so often don't say anything of value.

WRITING THE EMPLOYMENT SECTION

Although your Experience section will appear before your Employment section, most people find it easier to write about their hands-on work experience and education than about their abstracted skills and abilities. So begin writing about your jobs and education, then use this as your source of information for the Experience section.

You must tell the employer the most pertinent details of your duties and accomplishments for previous employers (or college studies, duties at home, volunteer work and so on). Sound obvious? Notice that this is different from listing your job description, what someone in the position usually does, or what you were "supposed" to have done in your position. *Tell the reader what you accomplished, improved upon, created, developed or sold, and if you excelled, to what degree compared to others in the field or company: "Ranked #1 in sales of ten employees," etc.*

Now it's time to start refining the information on your worksheets and the right side of the Personal Assessment sheet, get a clean sheet of paper and begin writing the text for your Employment section. Check the sentence starters in the Tipster below and scan the resume examples. Start with your most applicable information and list the following:

1. *Company or school name and location* (city and state only).
2. *Your job title with the organization (or college degree).* Keep this generic enough to be understood by managers at other firms. Keep it simple: "Staff Accountant," "Account Manager," "Senior Chemical Engineer," "Midwestern Sales Representative" and so on. Check the samples for more titles.
3. *Months and years at each position.* If you have gaps of more than three months between jobs, try using only years: 1986-1987, 1987-1992 and so on. Use whichever works best for you, but keep it consistent for all positions. List major responsibilities at each position and omit the trivial. You must think of what you do/did every day that helped contribute to bottom-line profitability or efficiency for the organization. See the following pages for a breakdown of responsibilities in some of the more common positions and apply these ideas to your career background.
4. *Your most important accomplishments with each company.* Include such items as exceeding sales quotas, reducing overhead, speeding response to customers, reducing mistakes in filing and order processing and so on. If positive, how did you rank among others in your company or college? Did you help streamline production activities? If this resulted in increased revenues, by how much over what period of time? See Chapter 5, "Outlines for the Major Professions," for further explanations. Did worker output improve under your management? If so, by how much and how quickly? Did your leadership help reduce turnover? By what percentage over what length of time? It's great to provide numbers to detail your success, but be sure to avoid making your resume a laundry list or heavy data sheet. Adding a return after each sentence adds white space within your text.

Talking out loud about your skills, duties and achievements will help you think and can make your writing much more understandable. Typically, you should offset these items below your primary duties with dashes, asterisks, or small bullets, as in the resume examples. These asterisks also help to break up gray blocks of type and add white space.

You should be able to do this without misrepresenting yourself and without using what I call *fluff* words or gibberish. If you can't, then perhaps you're not right for the position, or it's not right for you. Step back and take another look at your situation. Are your skills and abilities transferable to other fields or markets? Someone who's great at speech communications or English might also be great in sales, and many firms are willing to train newcomers in product lines, sales presentations and customer service.

Alternatively, a sales representative who is used to communicating with a wide range of people may be great in personnel as a recruiter. Teachers can become trainers; accountants can get into personal investment planning; secretaries can branch off into customer service, event planning or the travel industry, and so on. With additional training in the latest computer systems, the Internet and on-line services, more and more career doors open for highly motivated people, which includes you, right?

It's all a matter of how you present your talents related to the position at hand. A great resume must always:

1. Provide facts and/or data about your talents related to the position. This may be included in the Objective, Experience or Employment sections. Some resumes will have all three of these elements, while others work better without the first two.
2. Create an impression of organization, intelligence and increasing responsibility. It should build upon itself line after line.
3. Give an overall feeling that you know your profession and/or abilities extremely well, if such is the case, and can now use your talents in the employer's business environment. This is best accomplished in the Experience section by combining years of work skills, abilities, training and/or education in various aspects of the profession with the jargon of the trade. The Experience and Employment sections are the most important parts of your resume. For an inexperienced college graduate, it's the Experience and Education sections. It is essential to keep in mind the discriminating *employer's* point of view. Put yourself in his or her shoes and think about the employer's needs. Write to suit those needs, using information in the job posting whenever possible.

WRITING THE EXPERIENCE SECTION

The Experience section is used to group all your best and most currently marketable skills together. These skills are extracted from your past and, in some cases, taken out of context and sold to the reader. Use the information you have in front of you from the left side of your Personal Assessment sheet.

Groupings

Use bullet points to group like activities together. Accounting activities can be grouped with cost-effective purchasing, along with your knowledge of the hardware and software used in conducting your accounting (or secretarial or customer service, etc.) duties. Mention your level of knowledge in such terms as "familiar with," "trained in," "skilled in," "proficient in."

Describe your management and/or leadership skills: "Procedure planning and implementation" or "Coordinate budgets and inventories; assist in long- and short-term strategic planning." Mention the types of projects, operations and/or activities in which you've been involved.

Sales-related talents go well together: "Account prospecting, acquisition and management"; "Utilize demographic and direct mail sources in new market penetration; plan and conduct sales presentations in a professional manner; effectively train new sales representatives in product lines; determine and meet specific client needs"; and so on. Emphasize product lines or industries you wish to be associated with and omit those you would rather stay away from. Mention computer software and equipment used in account tracking, lead follow-up and management.

People skills should be presented together: "Skilled in staff hiring, training and supervision, group orientation and performance review"; "Plan and conduct training programs and seminars." "Assist in staff training and motivation in customer service and sales support"; "Train and coordinate human resource personnel in benefits administration and vacation scheduling."

There are five bullet points in the following example, which could be used to describe the world's most perfect worker. Use a maximum of three bullets for a one-page resume and five bullets for a two-pager:

EXPERIENCE:
- More than ten years in engineering, machine design and secondary tooling, including full responsibility for special projects.
- Proficient in AutoCad and familiar with EasyCad, as well as Lotus 1-2-3; skilled machinist, tool & die maker and welder: ARC and MIG.
- Handle cost-effective purchasing of parts and materials; skilled in vendor relations, price quoting, sales presentations and proposal writing.
- Skilled in equipment design and fabrication from concept to completion; experience with pneumatic & hydraulic systems & components, automation equipment and a full range of specialty products.

> • Plan and implement budgets with senior-level personnel; perform job/labor estimates and hire, train & supervise shop staff and managers.

The fastest, easiest way to change the focus of this resume for different positions is to rearrange the bullet points and print a new first page. An Experience section for a homemaker returning to, or entering, the work force could be:

EXPERIENCE: • **General Office Skills:** Accurate typist (45 wpm); familiar with WordPerfect 6.0, Quicken and 10-key calculators; experience with facsimile and photocopy machines.
• **Purchasing:** Experience in comparative shopping and cost-effective buying of clothing, food and appliances.
• **Filing and Bookkeeping:** Proven ability to balance monthly bank statements against checkbook entries for an active family of five; update and maintain all records related to income and real estate taxes on a 486 PC.

Don't worry about using the word *Experience* before this section. Even though it is not employment experience acquired from a paying job, it is life experience acquired through hard work, diligence, trial and error, and intellect. The resume is your chance to present all of this background in a business light and show that they are skills and abilities that could be applied to a paying position. Remember, if you don't like the word *Experience* here, use *Profile*.

☞ *Tipster . . .*

Here are some great sentence starters, phrases and qualifiers to jump-start your creativity and market your abilities in the Experience section:

Proven abilities in (list key areas of your profession) . . . More than (x) years in (if between 2 and 15 years) . . . Proficient in . . . Skilled in . . . Experience in . . . Extensive background in (or Qualifications in) . . . Plan and conduct . . . Compile and present . . . Hire, train and supervise staff in . . .

Especially for new college graduates, the newly trained or aspiring:

Familiar with . . . Trained in . . . Education in . . . Knowledge of . . . Assist in . . .

CHAPTER 5

Outlines for the Major Professions

According to a survey by the American Society of Training and Development, the top four qualities today's employer wants in workers are:

1. The ability to learn.
2. The ability to listen and convey information.
3. The ability to solve problems in innovative ways.
4. The knowledge of how to get things done.

All four of these points are best conveyed in your Profile or Experience section. Not by blurting them out in these words, but by using such phrases as "plan and implement," "research and analyze," "compile and present," "determine and meet specific customer needs," etc. Following are some key points to include for various professions, followed by some tips for college graduates and those without much work experience. These ideas apply to almost all professions but be sure to check the resume samples before writing.

ACCOUNTANTS

Try to present yourself as more than another number cruncher. Talk about participation in company or community activities. Interests in sporting events and hobbies should be placed near the bottom in a Personal section only if these activities don't appear so extensive as to detract from your work performance and if this alone won't take you into a second page.

Can you handle, manage, supervise, process, or are you trained in payroll processing, general ledgers, inventories, accounts payable, accounts receivable, billing, etc? If so, on what type of computer, using what type of software? Have you ever compiled and presented monthly, quarterly or annual reports (written, orally or both) or do you think you are able to? Did you assist in converting your company from a manual to a computerized system?

SALES REPRESENTATIVES

The Experience section is a great place to reinforce the best sales talents: "Account prospecting, acquisition and management"; "Determine and meet specific client needs"; "Plan and conduct written and oral presentations using audiovisual materials." Group your best skills in a general manner in the Experience section, then get specific about dollar volume and where you acquired and applied those skills through hands-on work experience and accomplishments at previous jobs.

The ability to meet or exceed quotas is an essential element in the sales representative's resume. Be sure to put this in perspective for the reader. How many other reps also made quota? In your office, your division, your state? Did you exceed your goals monthly, annually or quarterly? Did you receive any special performance awards? If so, explain exactly why you received them: "Earned Golden Pyramid Award for exceeding quota eight consecutive months." Did you ever train or orient new sales staff in territorial management, client relations or product demonstrations?

SYSTEMS ANALYSTS/COMPUTER PROGRAMMERS

Mention all computer-related knowledge but use qualifiers for levels of expertise. For instance: "proficient in/with," for software and hardware; "fluent in," for languages; and "familiar with," for anything about which you have only a cursory knowledge. Under Employment, mention projects, applications and accomplishments *specific to each position*.

Be as specific as possible. Mention all relevant hardware, software and programming languages in the Experience section and you won't have to repeat yourself quite so much. Under Employment, specify how your systems knowledge was applied (for what end result) under each particular job.

PHYSICIANS, ATTORNEYS, TEACHERS AND TOP EXECUTIVES

Here is where the Experience section can be kept extremely short, if not omitted completely. Trying to summarize briefly what these positions are about at the top of a resume is often pointless, because it will almost certainly be read by another physician, attorney, teacher or executive who should have a good grasp of your abilities based on your work history. Executives should include a two-bullet or three-bullet summary of how many years in the business (if not more than 15) and/or emphasize their areas of expertise, then follow with work experience and achievements under Employment.

SECRETARIES

The gutsy soldier of the working world and perhaps the most underpaid. The best secretaries have two big problems: giving themselves credit for—and writing about—the huge variety of work they do every day. Think of all the correspondence you write, type, collate, file, stamp, mail or ship overnight. Do you, or can you, write about meetings, legal matters, new office procedures, sales results or company events? List equipment you're proficient or familiar with: mailing and stamping machines, personal computers or word processors (list hardware and software), as well as brands and sizes of switchboards. State how fast you type (if 45 wpm or better) and mention "with accuracy" if true. Can you transcribe from a Dictaphone? Are you skilled in the use of 10-key calculators? Have you ever arranged travel itineraries or helped out in billing, customer service or other departments when they were too swamped? Would you say you can "provide sales support" to sales reps? Note your professional communication skills via telephone and in person, as well as any commendations received for outstanding performance.

ENGINEERS: MECHANICAL, ELECTRONIC AND CHEMICAL

Because these fields can be so wide ranging and diverse, expand upon projects and type of work you would like to see more of and downplay those you dislike. Mention applicable hardware, software and language proficiency, as well as product applications. Don't be afraid to get technical in your wording. Human resources staff may be omitted from the screening process for high-tech jobs, so write at a level your boss would appreciate. Provide details on projects supervised or improved upon, vendor sourcing, technical report writing, cost analyses, interfacing with internal or external technical staff, and presentations to clients. You can also name-drop some of your larger accounts if confidentiality is not a problem. For example, you might say: "Industrial accounts included Motorola, Intel and Microsoft." Or simply touch on this in your Experience section: "More than five years in product and process development, including project management (or system design) experience with Fortune 500 accounts."

Every profession cannot be reviewed here, so check resume examples that parallel your background. Many of these ideas are applicable to all types of jobs. If you lack traditional work experience, concentrate on skills acquired through education. Lacking education, you can emphasize talents and abilities acquired through volunteer work or other daily activities, such as basic home bookkeeping. You must present these in a business-like format.

NEW COLLEGE GRADUATES

New graduates should take full advantage of such qualifiers as "education in" or "training in" in their Profile or Experience section to show a certain level of knowledge in a given area: "Qualifications in human relations and team leadership" or "well versed in group dynamics and processes" (from fraternities, volunteer groups or projects); "Plan and conduct written and oral presentations in a professional manner; organize meetings, programs and events" (from class assignments and volunteer/community work).

Recently, I wrote a resume for a new college graduate who came into my office with the standard new grad's resume. After a brief Objective, the body of the text began with, you guessed it, his education. The very first line listed the name of his university and the month and year of his graduation. These resumes always look like advertisements for the school. Like every other new grad's resume, it's crying out to employers: "Help! I just graduated with a zillion other people who have little or no hands-on experience in my chosen field but hire me anyway!"

If you're a new college graduate, I beg you to use at least some kind of Profile or Experience section at the top of your resume. Put your lack of "experience" aside and tell the employer *what you learned* in all those classes you took and in all those volunteer groups, fraternities and special projects. Show how much you know about communication and how you can at least write a resume using powerful, businesslike language.

Be sure to see Gary L. Larson's resume on page 96, as well as the corresponding cover letter in Chapter 7. His Profile section was extracted from his employment *and* education experiences. This is the new graduate whose resume I rewrote and from the 20 laser prints he sent out, he received four interviews and four job offers. He also received compliments on his resume from interviewers. I told him to say thanks and act as if he wrote it himself.

Following a one- to three-bullet Profile section, in the Education section you can mention the subjects and lengths of any term papers related to the profession: "Conducted comprehensive interviews with engineers at the Zion nuclear power plant and wrote a 25-page report detailing safety procedures and apparatus for the prevention of full or partial core meltdowns." Under Experience, this would be summarized as "Handle research and report writing."

Dig for any other gems over the past four years: "Trained and supervised student volunteers for a campus recycling program and increased the volume of recycled newspapers by 35 percent"; "Directly involved in [or responsible for] proofreading and editing copy for the 1990 edition of the Campus-Times yearbook." Mention your GPA if it's within one point of a straight-A average: 3.0/4.0 or 4.0/5.0.

Be sure to mention whether that applies to your major or overall GPA. Don't make employers guess!

List any other campus activities, but try to avoid listing political groups or other affiliations that may draw the wrath of prejudice. Exceptions include fundraisers involving promotions or other business-like activities where you feel your organizational, communication or leadership talents are worth mentioning, despite the church or political group for which they were performed. As always, market your skills and achievements, then emphasize or downplay their context as required.

You can list relevant course titles, but it's even more important to include what was actually learned and accomplished. Did you attend extracurricular seminars, lectures or speeches? Conducted by whom and from what profession? Were you a member of business, computer or speech/literature clubs on campus? Was this membership valuable? What was your input? Think about everything you learned in those four years and how it can now be utilized in the everyday working world, because now you will be paid to communicate, analyze, react, manage, think and organize.

Marketing your acquired knowledge and talents as a new college graduate in this unique manner will distance your resume from the typical data sheet resume sent out every year by the millions.

HOMEMAKERS/HOUSEWIVES

Let's face it, there are no more housewives of the Laura Petrie type. Today's homemaker juggles his or her time between duties better phrased as budget planning, cost-effective purchasing, chauffeuring, child training and supervision, counseling, meal production and household maintenance. Double-check the Experience example above.

Like most effective marketing, it's all in the presentation. If you have absolutely no work history, a functional format may work best. Unless you have a specific job objective in mind, simply generalize about the type of position sought and be specific about the skills you can bring to an organization.

VETERANS RETURNING TO THE WORK FORCE

Veterans must do more than list the obvious, such as their rank, division name and locations of service. More than anyone else, they need to extract their abilities acquired from actual assignments and present them in a business light. This is essential for making those abilities appear applicable to the position they're seeking. I recommend either a functional or combination format with an Experience section outlining technical, management, human resource or clerical skills in general terms: "Handle system troubleshooting and repair to component level"; "Plan and conduct written and oral presentations; proven ability to determine and meet goals through effective staff training and supervision; update and maintain inventories, schedules and financial records." You must then reinforce this section with specific routines, maneuvers and/or duties performed for your unit.

You should also mention achievements, awards and commendations. Be sure to explain for what reason the medals or certificates were received, or it may seem meaningless to a civilian. Again, check the resume examples and use words and phrases that apply to you. Look under *Veterans* in the resume index in the back of this book.

BASIC VERSUS EFFECTIVE STATEMENTS

Here are examples of boring phrases turned into exciting statements for both the Experience and Employment sections. Break down your duties and highlight the key elements. Notice that it's all right to combine sentences in the same paragraph with a semicolon, as in the fourth *effective* sample below.

Basic	Effective
<u>EXPERIENCE Section:</u>	
Carefully review financial statements and handle a variety of general accounting duties.	Analyze profit/loss statements and maintain the accuracy of data related to payroll, AP/AR and delinquent accounts.
Update account prospect cards and provide full support to sales personnel.	Utilize ACT software in the tracking and updating of account prospect cards; provide full support to sales staff and compile weekly activity reports.
Buy equipment directly from manufacturers and utilize a computer to create support materials.	Experience in the cost-effective purchase of medical equipment and supplies [when product-specific]. Utilize Harvard Graphics to design and produce brochures and product spec sheets.
Plan sales ideas, hardware & software; work with programmers and technical staff.	Plan and implement creative sales concepts; develop specialized hardware and software promotions through interface with programmers and technical staff.
<u>EMPLOYMENT Section:</u>	
Supervise 14 Sales Representatives in the Southern U.S.	Effectively hire, train and supervise a staff of 14 in key account prospecting, acquisition and management in a large Southern territory.
Wrote an employee manual covering numerous important topics.	Performed in-depth research and wrote a comprehensive employee manual outlining worker benefits, disciplinary/probationary procedures and corporate philosophy.
Responsible for customer service and the supervision of sales staff.	Interfaced with restaurant owners, managers and construction contractors to meet specific equipment needs. Conducted sales presentations, developed budgets and trained/supervised personnel.
Operated a cash register and sold merchandise.	Handled effective customer service and the operation of a NEC computerized register at this high-volume drugstore.

POWER/ACTION WORDS

Use these words to add power and impact to your writing:

Accelerated	Contracted	Fulfilled	Organized
Accomplished	Contributed	Generated	Overhauled
Achieved	Controlled	Guided	Oversaw
Acquired	Converted	Handled	Participated
Adapted	Coordinated	Headed (up)	Performed
Administered	Corrected	Helped	Pinpointed
Advanced	Created	Hired	Pioneered
Advised	Cut	Identified	Planned
Allocated	Decreased	Implemented	Prepared
Amended	Defined	Improved	Presented
Analyzed	Delegated	Improvised	Prevented
Applied	Delivered	Increased	Processed
Appointed	Demonstrated	Initiated	Procured
Approved	Designed	Innovated	Produced
Assessed	Determined	Instituted	Programmed
Assigned	Developed	Inspected	Projected
Assisted	Devised	Instructed	Promoted
Attained	Directed	Integrated	Proposed
Audited	Discovered	Interpreted	Proved
Averted	Distributed	Interviewed	Provided
Avoided	Documented	Introduced	Published
Broadened	Doubled	Invented	Purchased
Budgeted	Drafted	Investigated	Realized
Built	Earned	Launched	Recommended
Calculated	Edited	Lectured	Recruited
Centralized	Eliminated	Liquidated	Redesigned
Clarified	Enforced	Located	Reduced
Collected	Engineered	Made	Regulated
Combined	Established	Maintained	Reinforced
Compiled	Evaluated	Managed	Reorganized
Completed	Executed	Marketed	Reported
Computed	Expanded	Minimized	Represented
Conceived	Expedited	Modified	Researched
Condensed	Extracted	Monitored	Resolved
Conducted	Financed	Motivated	Restored
Consolidated	Focused	Negotiated	Restructured
Constructed	Forecasted	Obtained	Reversed
Consulted	Formulated	Operated	Reviewed
Contained	Founded	Ordered	Revised

Revitalized	Solved	Surpassed	Trained
Revived	Spearheaded	Surveyed	Trimmed
Saved	Specified	Sustained	Undertook
Scheduled	Streamlined	Tabulated	Unified
Screened	Strengthened	Tailored	Updated
Secured	Structured	Taught	Validated
Set up	Studied	Terminated	Wrote
Shaped	Supervised	Tested	
Simplified	Supported	Tightened	

CHAPTER 6

Notes on Format and Printing

TRICKS OF THE TRADE

Laser typesetting or professional printing is the best way to produce your resume. If you really must use a typewriter, you can still make those nice "bullets" for your Experience section. It's done by using the small "o" and filling it in with a fine-point pen. Ball point pens leave white spots, so make sure you use a small felt tip with black ink. I recommend hanging the bullet out in the margin as in the example below, but you may also rest it above the second line of copy.

Bullet points work well because they make your talents quickly digestible. They break up gray blocks of type, attract the eye and provide a focal point, which is followed by your most applicable skills and abilities. Remember, your resume must now be future oriented rather than dwell on the past:

EXPERIENCE:
- More than five years in sales and marketing, including full responsibility for account acquisition, cost analysis, product installation and client relations.
- Effectively hire, train and supervise technical staff in system analysis, programming and data processing.
- Fluent in Fortran and BASIC; familiar with COBOL, PASCAL, PL/1 and UNIX.

To add variety, you may also use a simple dash or asterisk:

- Proven ability to increase bottom-line sales through demographic research, targeted direct mail campaigns and cold calling competitors' accounts.
* Perform field staff hiring, training and supervision; plan and conduct seminars on sales techniques, product lines and potential markets.

Use frills like bold facing, underlining, italics, bullets or dashes *sparingly.* Use them only to make major points stand out or to set items apart and break up type. They quickly lose their impact when overused. Avoid using bold facing, underlining and italics in the same resume; choose a combination of any two. My personal favorites are bolding and underlining, but pick whichever you prefer.

If your full name has fewer than 15 letters, you can center your name at the top of the page and make it appear larger just by adding a space between letters:

R O B E R T E. J O N E S

rather than

ROBERT E. JONES

At first glance, some of these techniques may seem simplistic. Yet that is why so few people think of using them and find themselves with yet another boring data-sheet resume that doesn't work. Combining these techniques will help you stand out in the crowd.

MARGINS AND LINE LENGTH

Most resume examples in this guide follow a simple, conservative format. The body copy is almost always indented about 1.5 inches from the left margin. This allows for shorter lines and makes the resume more scannable, reducing reader fatigue. This also gives greater white space and an excellent place to put your Objective, Experience and other headings. Margins should be 1 inch all around, but they may be shortened to ¾ inch or widened up to 1.5 inches as needed to fit your background neatly on one page—if you don't have enough information to start a second page. If you still need more or less space than margin shifting allows, change your type size by ½ to 1 point, but try to keep it at or near 11 points.

Hyphenate words at the end of lines to avoid violating your margins. However, you can make an exception to this rule for compound words such as self-employed, and end the line after *self-.* You should square-off, or fully justify your lines if space is tight. Note that most resumes in this guide are fully justified, in order to pack more information on each page, but that there is almost always a return at the end of each individual sentence. This automatically adds white space between lines, helping us avoid large blocks of gray type.

If you would like to hide employment gaps of three to four months, go ahead and use only years, but be prepared to back this up when asked. I prefer placement of dates directly across from job title or company name, flush right. An Assistant Director for Alumni Career Services at a major university said she liked to see dates placed immediately after the company location: "Chicago, IL, 8/93-1/9." I agree with this if you'd like to hide or mask dates of shorter positions. Besides, you want employers to focus on your abilities and experience, not dates.

You should begin your Employment descriptions with whichever title is most impressive and *applicable* to the position you are seeking. For example:

EMPLOYMENT:	The State Department, Washington, D.C.	3/92-Present
	Assistant Computer Operator	
However:	**Chief Executive Officer**	
	Domino's Pizza, Omaha, NE	4/91-Present
Or:	**The Pentagon,** Washington, D.C.	9/90-Present
	Maintenance Worker	

You should still underline Maintenance Worker here because it clearly separates it from the copy that follows. When dates are tucked in at the right margin, you leave the left margin clear and allow for more white space.

Optical Centering

The optical center of a resume, a portrait or just about anything is roughly a third down from the top of the page. It's where the eye likes to look and that's where your Experience section will be:

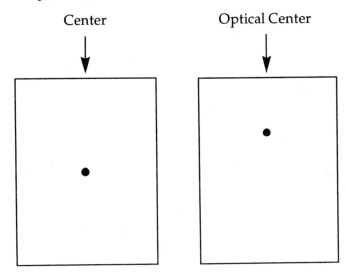

WHAT COLOR PAPER TO USE

In just about all cases, white, off-white, or ivory linen paper is best. Avoid dark grays, blues or browns. Although these darker colors can reduce glare from office lights, they also reduce contrast between paper and ink. Executives can use a light gray for a very conservative look, but lighter paper works better when your resume is faxed to an employer or scanned for use on a database (more on scanned resumes later). Avoid the splotchy parchment papers used by the large resume companies. Consider Classic Linen Writing in Solar White or Baronial Ivory, 24 lb.; Beckett Linen in various colors; and one of the smoother papers, Strathmore Wove, in natural or white.

WHAT TYPEFACE AND SIZE

There are two basic styles of type: serif and sans serif. Serifs are the "tips" and "feet" at the top and bottom of letters. Almost every major newspaper uses serif type. What you are reading now is 11 point Palatino. Here are examples of serif and sans serif type:

This typeface is called Times Roman (or just Times) in 11 pt.
This is Times Roman in 10 pt. This is Times Roman in 12 pt.
This is called Courier in 10 pt. and is similar to a common typewriter font.
This is called Helvetica in 11 pt.

Keep your typeface between 10.5 and 12.5 pts. If it fits well on the page, 11.5 pt. is recommended. Use 12.5 to 13 pt. type only when necessary to fill the page, or if you expect your resume to be scanned onto an electronic resume network (more on this later). Anything smaller is hard for the eye to scan and anything larger can look childish.

As for choosing between serif or sans serif types, serif types are recommended for most professions. They are easy to read, conservative and fairly common. If you are in a creative or high-tech field (e.g, computer science, advertising, graphic arts or aerospace), a more modern sans serif type, such as Helvetica or Kent, is recommended.

If you must use a typewriter, make sure it has a plastic, one-time ribbon rather than an old cloth carbon ribbon. The difference in clarity is substantial and the reproduction quality of masters printed on some of the newer typewriters can come close to that of laser printers and typesetting. Such machines may feature bold facing, interchangeable daisy print wheels and lift-off correction ribbons.

You can create a great resume master on a typewriter and have it reproduced on a high-quality photocopier at a fraction of the cost of typesetting at a print shop. This is recommended only if you need to save money and have access to good equipment. The typewriter should have proportional spacing, a feature that emulates typesetting because it actually packs the letters together, side by side. All typefaces used in this text are proportional except those in Courier, which appears spread out across the page.

Laser Printing

Try to get actual laser prints of your resume, rather than just photocopies, on your choice of paper.

If you can't find a good resume service or a good typewriter or computer and laser printer at your local library, call the printers in your area. For $35 to $40, they should be able to laser typeset your resume and give you at least 25 photocopies of a one-page format.

Before accepting your final prints, proofread your resume slowly and carefully. Be sure to check everything, including dates of employment and the spelling of company names and your name, address and phone number.

This book is about writing your resume yourself and you should be able to come close to a professional writer's quality using the tips presented here. Typing your resume on an excellent typewriter with boldfacing, proportional spacing and lift-off correction ribbon can save you over $200 for a two-page resume.

Don't forget resume services or secretarial/word processing services. They can key your resume onto a computer disk and laser print a master copy, which you then take to a copy shop. Corrections and updates are then quick, easy and economical.

☞ *Tipster . . .*

Beware of the black lines and gray streaks characteristic of many photocopies. These can sometimes be removed by lightening the exposure, but if you can't find a copier that works to your satisfaction, take your document to a resume service for laser originals or photocopies. Remember, this is your life, your career on paper and one of the best investments you can make. It must appear clean and crisp, with no clutter and as close to perfect as possible. You wouldn't wear a shabby suit to an interview, would you? Don't use a shabby resume! Take your time to get it done right, with or without professional assistance.

FORMATTING FOR ELECTRONIC RESUME NETWORKS

Electronic resume networks can be an excellent way to distribute your resume, especially if you would like to relocate to a new region. Basically, you can fax, modem or mail your resume to a firm that scans/lists your information on a database for a fee. Potential employers then log on to the database (for another fee) and review your background. Employers may conduct targeted searches for applicants according to geographic preference, skills, abilities, employment background and education.

Such databases are beginning to catch on with employers because they save recruiters time and search for resumes with certain key words or phrases, such as market research, sales, staff training or management, accounting, programming, compensation management, policy development, typing, customer service, AS 400 or Lotus 1-2-3. Again, these words are quantified and qualified with lead-ins such as skilled in, trained in, proficient in, etc. Fortunately, if you write a good Combination resume, these key words will appear in the Experience section and some will also be used to relate to specific job duties (e.g., supervise 12 employees in . . .) under Employment.

When creating your resume, format a scannable version and keep it as current as your standard one. Because computers aren't perfect and cannot "read" like the human eye, follow these tips when producing a scannable resume:

1. Use a standard typeface in 12-point type or larger. Times or Courier should work well.
2. Omit italics, underlines and decorative graphics. Some scanners can read bold facing, but play it safe and avoid this too.
3. Use standard 8½ × 11-inch paper in white or off-white. This increases the contrast between ink and paper and works better on scanners.
4. Scanned or not, never fold your resume. Toner from laser printers or copiers can actually crack off the page, leaving incomplete type, black dust and a terrible mess.
5. Send an original of your resume from a laser or ink-jet printer, not a photocopy. Use a modem to send your resume whenever possible, and consider sending it on disk, in ASCII format as well as your word processor's format.
6. Remember to use jargon of the trade and as many key words as possible, like those listed above. Give the computer what it wants.
7. Don't indent any lines. That's right. Keep a straight left-hand margin. You can stack titles above paragraphs such as:

EMPLOYMENT: **1991-Present**
MANAGER, Motorola, Inc., Schaumburg, IL
Responsible for training and supervising engineers building self-destruct capability for all "Star Wars" defense systems. Through detailed analyses, lowered the cost of transistors and components 15%.

One large resume database is the Worldwide Resume/Talent Bank, and Online Solutions, Inc., provides access for uploading resumes to that databank. I first heard about this through America Online's Career Center forum. Online Solutions can upload your resume and make it available to all users of the Internet, including many employers worldwide. They use OCR (Optical Character Recognition) to scan your resume onto their computers. Once that's complete, your resume can be searched by anyone with access to the database, including all America Online (AOL) users at no extra charge. As of April 1995, this database had 20,000 resumes and it's still growing. This particular database is accessed via the Online Career Center on the Internet for a viewing audience of 43 million.

According to Wayne Gonyea, "Other resume databases have been developed by a myriad of associations, groups and companies. They vary widely in size, content, accessibility and cost. Their primary commonality is that they are all searched in one way or another by computers.

"On the far end of the spectrum are resume management systems. These systems scan resumes into data bases, search the databases on command, and rank the resumes according to the number of resulting 'hits' they receive. Such resume management systems are usually utilized by major corporations and recruitment firms. The reliance upon resume management systems, coupled with the downsizing of human resource departments in many corporations, has resulted in a situation whereby *many resumes are never seen by human eyes once they enter the electronic systems!*

"The lesson, therefore, is to make the resume as computer/scanner friendly as possible so that its life in a database will be extended and its likelihood of producing 'hits' is enhanced. We put in full-text resumes on the Worldwide Resume/Talent Bank, so every word of the resume is included."

Our company, *A ADVANCED* Resume Service, Inc., charges $35 to upload your resume for worldwide access. Resumes can be updated and remain on the database for one year, after which they are automatically deleted.

CHAPTER 7

Cover Letters

Your cover letter is an essential part of your job search and should be tailored and targeted to individual employers whenever possible. When you know the name of the company and person to whom you will be sending your resume, then a cover letter is essential. Here you can state more specifically what type of work you're applying for, which is especially valuable if you omitted an Objective on your resume. It also gives you the chance to write less formally about who you are, what you can accomplish in the position and what you know about the firm. This last item can really help separate you from the crowd. You must research the firm whenever possible and demonstrate that you know:

1. Something, *anything* special about the products or services they produce.
2. Their target markets: business, general consumer, national or international.
3. Their current hiring needs and how you can help fill those needs.

ESSENTIAL POINTS OF THE COVER LETTER

Your cover letter should contain:

1. The exact title of the position you are seeking. If that's not possible, then the general type of work for which you are applying.
2. Why you want to work for the company.
   Keep answering that question: "What can you do for me?"
3. A decent sample of what you know about the company's product lines, marketing strategies, quality and quantity of clientele, and where they stand among their competitors. For example: "I understand you will be introducing your new Sextant computer chip in the Japanese market

this Fall. I have several ideas that may help you compete with Intel's established line."

Obviously, not everyone wants to be in sales or product management, but you get the picture. Be sure to check annual reports at the library and the latest newspaper and magazine articles and trade journals, even *The Nightly Business Report* or *Wall Street Week* on television. All sources can prove valuable in your research, especially former coworkers or people at professional associations.

4. You may include "Willing to travel or relocate for the right opportunity," if this is a factor related to the line of work, such as outside sales or consulting. Omit this if it is not requested or if you are not willing to travel or relocate.

5. Any other specific items about yourself or the job. If the posting says: "Include salary requirements" and not salary history, give them a desired salary range and avoid a specific number. For example, "upper $30s per year, negotiable." You may include this in a letter, but if they ask for salary requirements *and* salary history, include them on a separate salary history sheet and end the page with "Salary requirements are open to negotiation." See the salary history example in Chapter 8.

IMPORTANT DETAILS TO GET YOUR LETTER READ

1. Send a cover letter with your resume and personalize it by first researching the company and, whenever possible, getting the name of the hiring authority. Make sure to get the correct spelling. Exceptions can be made for blind box ads, but if it looks like an exceptional position, then by all means include a letter addressed to "Ladies/Gentlemen:," "Dear Hiring Authority:" or "Dear Prospective Employer:". Use a colon (:) when you've never spoken to the individual and a comma when you have.

   See the back of this book for resource materials available from your local library.

2. If you can't get the name of a hiring authority, send it to the personnel manager, human resources representative, or corporate recruiter, with the person's name, if possible.

3. Make your letters brief and to the point and they stand a better chance of getting read. Remember that some employers skip the letter entirely and get to it only after they like what they see in your resume, so keep your letter down to three or four short paragraphs to increase its readability. Other employers rely heavily on a well-written, customized cover letter, so take the time to do it right.

4. Cover letters should be laser printed or typed. Try to match paper colors of resumes and letters, but don't worry too much about this. Plain white

goes well with everything, is easy to correct on your typewriter and doesn't look mass produced. It also looks more personal and immediate. If you honestly have *no way* of getting a letter typed, dictate to someone with great handwriting.

5. Proofread your letter as closely as your resume. Proofread once for content, then once for grammar and typing mistakes. Read each word individually from the bottom to the top and have your friends and family read it, too.

☞ *Tipster . . .*

During a lecture on resume writing, a member of the audience mentioned a special phone number at the U.S. Post Office to call for the names of companies running blind (P.O. Box only) advertisements in newspapers. Call your local post office to see if they can provide such information. If the P.O. Box is for the newspaper, which then routes resumes to specific companies, then this number won't work. Otherwise, you can research the company and target your cover letter.

If you call the company for information, keep in mind that one reason they run blind ads is to avoid such calls.

The cover letter should help generate interest in you and the resume that follows. You then close by requesting an interview, or better yet, telling the reader when you will be calling to arrange an interview. Personal contact shows you're aggressive and interested in that firm specifically.

Call the firm on the date you mail your cover letter and resume and try to speak directly with the manager or hiring authority. If that's impossible, at least talk to the personnel representative. Tell him or her your name and that you've sent a resume in application for the position. Try to begin a conversation about your qualifications and how you're just right for the job. But don't oversell yourself if the person sounds too busy to talk. Of course, if the advertisement or posting says, "No calls please," then don't call—unless you can anonymously learn the hiring authority's name and/or title from the receptionist. Then you can try calling that person directly and inquire about opportunities in your field, as if you've never seen the ad and as if you heard about the company through a friend or contacts in the industry. Practice this scenario first and be well prepared to handle yourself if you try this!

Call the company three to four days after sending your resume and try to speak with the actual hiring authority. Keep a detailed list or card file of resumes sent, to whom and on what date. Tell people you want to confirm that they've received your resume and that you would like to arrange an interview. Try to speak directly with the manager or supervisor, but if that's impossible, try the personnel representative. Be sure not to make a pest of yourself. Bothering anyone on the telephone can make you appear pushy and desperate.

As a corporate personnel representative, I came across an extreme example of this with an applicant whom the manager and I had already interviewed. We agreed that although the candidate had energy and some degree of experience, it just wasn't the kind of experience we thought was essential to the job. After learning he had not been hired, the applicant called our office at least ten times over the next two weeks to tell us more about his background and why he thought we had a great company. He drove the receptionist crazy and confirmed our suspicions of immaturity.

If the hiring authority or personnel representative refuses to speak with you or set an interview, call them once more the next day or two. If you're still very interested in the position, send a follow-up letter like the example in Chapter 8. Don't be discouraged by the standard "We're reviewing the applications and will be arranging interviews as soon as we've screened them all." This is the standard "Don't call us, we'll call you." And it is often justified. Sometimes employers really do want to sift through resumes first and then decide whom to meet.

The main reason for a personal resume follow-up is to drop your name into the mind of the manager or representative and distance yourself from the silent stack of resumes. If you can set an interview, fine. But remember that employers have time constraints and perhaps hundreds of resumes to screen, so don't be dismayed no matter how long it takes. I've heard of clients being called for interviews months after their resume was sent. Of course, they continued their job hunt at full speed during that time.

Don't be one of those people who approach the job search with a *me against them* attitude, *them* being the prospective employer. These people focus on the indifference of hiring managers and human resource staff. As hard as it may seem, you must always project yourself as an ally to all staff and managers at the target company. Act like you're already part of their operation. Try to create a *we* scenario without being presumptuous. Remember, these are people you may soon be working with.

☞ *Tipster . . .*

When mailing your resume and cover letter, be sure to use 9" × 12" envelopes that open on the long side. This keeps your resume flat and presentable, avoiding the "accordion" look of folded resumes. More importantly, folding along a line of text can actually crack the type off certain papers and the reader gets black toner all over the place.

Yes, this method raises your postage to 55 cents, (one 32-cent and one 23-cent stamp), but it's worth it. Next to a stack of #10 envelopes, yours stands out even before it's opened and is much easier to read. This is especially recommended for two- to three-page presentations with cover letters.

Chapter 8

Examples: Cover Letters and Follow-Up Letters, Reference and Salary History Sheets

SUSAN FIELD
671 Stearns Road
Bartlett, IL 60103
708/555-3574

Dear Hiring Manager:

With my diverse experience in human resource management and administration, I am exploring new opportunities with your company. The following resume outlines many key points of my background.

I believe it's been my ability to communicate on a personal, yet professional level with all staff and management that has helped me create a positive team environment at Canberra Electronics. It is here that I've developed and improved complete human resource management systems. Other achievements include instituting Employee Assistance Programs, improved staff training, a creative newsletter and a wide range of affirmative action and staffing programs.

Although my employment with Canberra has been highly successful, the Itasca office will soon be closed and operations will be moved to our Boston headquarters. Therefore, I would now like to explore opportunities with your company.

I have excellent letters of reference from Canberra and would be happy to provide any further information you require. Please let me know as soon as possible when we may meet for a personal interview, or to answer any questions you may have.

Sincerely yours,

Susan Field

encl.

INDUSTRY-SPECIFIC COVER LETTER

GEORGE RACER
1141 East Woodhollow Lane
Omaha, NE 40103
708/555-4581

Dear Hiring Manager:

Are you interested in a hard worker with a solid record of loyalty and dedication? I am seeking to utilize my education and skills in the Travel Industry.

If your company requires a team player with strong sales skills, dedication to customer service, accuracy and the ability to handle a high volume of phone calls, I believe I'm the right person for the job. My previous employment has required all of these skills.

Courses at Elgin Community College in travel and tourism have given me skills in Apollo reservations, ticketing and geography. Extra courses in business communication and keyboarding have further expanded my abilities.

If the brief description of my skills on the enclosed resume demonstrates that I meet your requirements, I would like an interview to discuss mutual interests. Please let me know as soon as possible when we may meet.

Thank you for your time and consideration.

Sincerely,

George Racer

encl.

FRANK B. THOMAS
2261 Gate Circle South
Hanover Park, ND 30103
317/555-4294

Dear Hiring Manager:

In this uncertain economy, even in the best managed companies, there is a growing consensus that experienced manufacturing talent will prove key to profitable operations throughout the 1990s.

Through 15 years of success, I've demonstrated a consistent ability to contribute to profitability in all areas of production, process engineering and leadership.

- As Plant Manager for a specialty metal products company, I've been instrumental in managing growth from $5 million to more than $20 million in a relatively short period. However, for reasons that I would be happy to share privately, I am looking to explore some new challenges.

Because I feel that your situation is one where my experience would fit nicely, I decided to forward my resume. If you feel it merits at least an exploratory discussion, I would be happy to arrange a visit at your convenience.

Thank you in advance for your consideration, and I look forward to hearing from you.

Sincerely,

Frank B. Thomas

encl.

JEFFREY H. CROCKETT
2245 Stephen Road
Aldona, CA 40089
213/555-3086

Ms. Shelly Cloud
Cloud Marketing, Inc.
1135 Washington Drive
Chicago, IL 60690

Dear Ms. Cloud:

Given the excellent reputation of your firm, [or Cloud Marketing/company name] I am submitting my resume in application for an Account Management position. Specifically, I am seeking to utilize my profit-building skills in account prospecting, acquisition and management to expand your company's profitability.

* In my position with Arty Incentives, I have proven my ability to create highly profitable, personalized relationships with key clientele at hundreds of companies. I've executed complex sales with a strong knowledge of product lines [you could list several here], industry trends and, of course, the customer's specific needs.

* My success thus far is the result of comprehensive research and taking an interactive role in a client's business. This allows me to design and implement customized incentive programs while always keeping a sharp eye on bottom-line results.

I am willing to travel [and/or relocate] for the right opportunity, and can provide excellent references at your request. Please let me know as soon as possible when we may meet for a personal interview [or: I will be contacting you soon to arrange a personal interview]. Thank you for your time and consideration.

Sincerely,

Jeffrey H. Crockett

encl.

EDWARD R. HOUND
2251 Texas Court
Addison, VT 40101
208/555-7215

Dear Hiring Manager:

With more than 12 years in Manufacturing and Design Engineering, I would like to discuss how my experience can benefit your company. I most recently read about your company's acquisition of Dilmer, Inc., a former client of my employer, GS Gibson.

► I currently manage a design and manufacturing engineering team in state-of-the-art product and process development for a wide range of applications. I would be most valuable in a position requiring greater innovation and creativity, and which offers the potential for career advancement.

► My efforts have resulted in major cost reductions and quality improvements for key customers, as well as for in-house operations. I can now assist your technical staff in virtually all stages of process and product development.

There is much more information I could provide, including a portfolio of photographs of my most important work. I look forward to hearing from you soon so we can discuss mutual interests.

Sincerely,

Edward R. Hound

encl.

REFERRED BY COMPANY EMPLOYEE

SHIRLEY MONROE
1162 Gravel Court
Lexington, KY 20139
608/555-2515

Cooper Norman
Vice President
Total Power Corporation
1400 S. Madison Street
Burr Ridge, IL 60521

Dear Mr. Norman:

I am exploring opportunities as Administrative Assistant and heard about your company through Jennifer Leigh, who suggested I send you my resume.

- I am a skilled typist, and proficient in WordPerfect 5.1 and Lotus 1-2-3. As my resume indicates, I have highly successful experience in the medical field and with Montgomery Ward's insurance division.

- Throughout my career, I've proven my ability to work effectively with management and staff at all levels of experience. Most importantly, I can ensure high customer satisfaction through personalized, yet highly effective communications.

- I thrive in the type of fast-paced environment where attention to detail and composure are essential to customer satisfaction and referral business.

I am eager to join your highly successful team of professionals. Please let me know as soon as possible when we may meet for an interview and discuss mutual interests. I look forward to your response.

Thank you for your time and consideration.

Sincerely,

Shirley Monroe

encl.

Mary Rodriquez
2452 Juniper Circle
Streamwood, IL 60196
708/555-8976

Ladies/Gentlemen:

1.   In the interest of seeking a position as Teacher with DePaul Language Academy, I have enclosed my resume for your review. It outlines my Teaching experience with learning disabled and normal students in Chicago and the suburbs.

2.   As the mother of an LD student and two college-bound students, I have proven my ability to work effectively with parents of students at virtually all aptitude levels.

3.   Throughout my career, I've demonstrated a strong devotion to teaching and my desire to work with students on a daily basis has never been greater. Former class activities have included full production supervision for the Rolling Knolls High School Year Book and I would be very interested in volunteer work with DePaul's After School Program.

Please contact me directly to arrange an interview, or for further information. Thank you for your time and consideration, and I look forward to great success with the students at [name of the school].

Sincerely,

Mary Rodriquez

encl.

NOTES: (1) This is a unique letter because Mary was presenting her qualifications directly to a committee for full-time status where she was currently a substitute. She was applying in Chicago where she had very little work experience, so I listed Chicago before suburbs. (2) It's all right to use LD after spelling out learning disabled in the first paragraph. Mentioning her children shows she has actual experience raising an LD child. (3) This shows a genuine interest in extracurricular activities and a background in the school's proposed program.

COVER LETTER: NEW COLLEGE GRADUATE WITH GENERAL OBJECTIVE

GARY L. LARSON
1121 Wicka Road
Heartland, WI 53029
414/555-5892

Dear Hiring Manager:

I am exploring opportunities with your company. Specifically, I am seeking to better utilize my ability to train, motivate and energize both groups and individuals in successful endeavors.

- During various volunteer positions in college, I was highly successful in training and coordinating individuals with a wide range of backgrounds. My hands-on work experience includes customer service, sales and business administration, all with a highly positive attitude.

- I've proven my ability to work effectively with management and staff at all levels of experience. Most importantly, I have demonstrated my ability to determine and meet the needs of the customer in a professional, yet personalized manner.

I can provide excellent references upon request, and am willing to travel for the right opportunity. Please let me know as soon as possible when we may meet for an interview and discuss mutual interests. I look forward to your response.

Thank you for your time and consideration.

Sincerely,

Gary L. Larson

encl.

GENERAL BOILERPLATE LETTER

THOMAS D. FLANDERS

223 Whitewood Drive
Arlington Heights, IL 60004
708/555-5134

Dear Hiring Executive [or Manager]:

I am exploring the possibility of joining your staff and have enclosed my resume for your review. Specifically, I would like to better utilize my talents in [sales/marketing, staff training, general accounting, production operations, etc.].

Throughout the challenges of my career, I've worked effectively with management and staff at all levels of experience. Most importantly, I have demonstrated my ability to determine and meet the needs of the customer with tact and professionalism.

My background includes full responsibility for [account prospecting, sales presentations and effective client relations], and this is the type of experience I can now bring to your company. I've developed excellent contacts at hundreds of large and small businesses, and I feel this can be extremely valuable to your firm.

I am available for an interview at your convenience to discuss how my education and experience could benefit you. Please contact me at the above number or address in order to arrange a meeting. I am looking forward to meeting you and discussing mutual interests.

Thank you for your time and consideration.

Sincerely,

Thomas D. Flanders

encl.

Alfred E. Plate
174 South East Avenue
Chicago, IL 60691
312/555-9276

PROFESSIONAL / EXECUTIVE
BOILER PLATE COVER LETTER

[**Note:** If name or title is not available,
you may use Ladies/Gentlemen, Dear Hiring
Manager or Dear Prospective Employer]

Mr. Bart Dennison
Director of Product Development
Snicker Corporation
129 LaSalle Street, Suite 12
Chicago, IL 60606

Dear Mr. Dennison:

The position of [position name] advertised in last Sunday's [newspaper name] seems tailor-made for me. My experience with [last or current employer] involved responsibility for [several duties listed in the ad], and my efforts resulted in a 20 percent reduction in overhead for 1989. The enclosed resume outlines my qualifications and accomplishments.

I now wish to apply my [supervisory/design/organizational, etc.] skills with an industry leader such as [company name, if applicable]. I am willing to travel or relocate and my salary requirements are negotiable. [You may omit "negotiable" and give a range, such as "upper $40s per year," if requested in the ad.]

I will contact you during the first week of August [or *soon*] to arrange an interview. Meanwhile, please feel free to give me a call should you require any further information on my background.

Sincerely,

Alfred E. Plate

encl.

BOILERPLATE COVER LETTER: INDUSTRY-SPECIFIC

GRAHAM CLEESE
246 Gregory Street
Glendale Heights, IL 60139
708/555-9363

Dear Hiring Manager:

In the interest of joining your company, I'm enclosing a resume outlining my experience in system analysis, programming and technical support.

My most important skills have been developed with Vantis corporation, a partnership between IBM and Sears Roebuck. It is here that I have learned how to deal with a wide range of problems and the people who present them, and to do so with speed and accuracy.

However, I feel that my ability to communicate well with a wide range of technical and nontechnical staff has been the key to my success. It is this ability I can now bring to your company, to further improve your customer service as well as your computer operations.

I am willing to travel or relocate for the right opportunity, and can provide solid references at your request. Please let me know as soon as possible when we may meet for an interview and discuss mutual interests. I look forward to your response.

Thank you for your time and consideration.

Sincerely,

Graham Cleese

encl.

Lucy Fatima
876 College Avenue
DeKalb, IL 60115
815/555-2474

BOILER PLATE COVER LETTER
BLIND AD / ENTRY LEVEL

Dear Prospective Employer [or Dear Hiring Manager]:

In the interest of exploring employment opportunities with your organization, I've enclosed my resume for your review. I am certain my experience [and training] in [office management, accounting, data processing, etc.] can help your company achieve greater profitability.

My strong work ethic and attention to detail would prove extremely valuable to a company that makes customer service its top priority. I am self-motivated and energetic, and communicate well with customers, fellow staff and management to get the job done.

Please let me know as soon as possible when we may meet to discuss mutual interests. Thank you for your time, and I look forward to your response.

Sincerely,

Lucy Fatima

encl.

RESUME FOLLOW-UP LETTER

WILLIAM STRUNC
4032 Golf Road
Roselle, AL 21017
438/555-8888

[Send this follow-up letter 7 to 10 days after sending your resume if you receive no response.]

Ladies/Gentlemen [or person's Name/Title, Dear Hiring Manager, Human Resources Representative, etc.]:

Last week I sent you a resume and cover letter in application for the position of [Mechanic, Driver, Sales Representative, etc.]. This letter is to confirm your receipt my resume, as well as my very strong interest in your company.

My hands-on experience and education would prove highly valuable to your operation. Because my resume and cover letter can only provide a brief explanation of my background, I would welcome the chance to meet with you personally to discuss your particular business needs. To that end, I look forward to hearing from you soon.

Thank you again for your time and consideration.

Sincerely,

William Strunc

RUSSELL G. BRUZEK
442 Commonwealth Court
Barrington, IL 60010-3154
708/555-2699

Mr. Charles Thicker   6/19/95
Production Manager
TCI CABLE
117 Northwest Hwy.
Park Ridge, IL 60068

Dear Charles:

I enjoyed speaking with you last week about the opportunity as Infomercial Producer at your Mt. Prospect studio.

The position seems perfect for me, as I have comprehensive experience in T.V. and film production, as well as in sales and marketing. I also have acting experience and am very skilled in coordinating talent and production teams. I work equally well with business leaders and those who've never appeared before on television.

After listening to Will Rodgers at the Cable Day presentation, I am convinced of the strong demand for advertising in the Infomercial format on cable T.V.

Please let me know as soon as possible when we may meet to discuss this further, or if there's any more information you require on my background.

Thanks for your time and consideration, Charles.

Yours,

Russell G. Bruzek

INTERVIEW FOLLOW-UP LETTER

Susan Winter
122 Arizona Blvd.
Redbrook, IL 60062
707/555-1265

[Note: The day after your interview, send
a note like this, or call your interviewer
to restate your interest in the position
and thank him/her for the interview.]

Betty Onassis
Regional Sales Manager
Cyrix Corporation
2139 Bluechip Drive
Chicago, IL 60683

Dear Ms. Onassis,

Thank you for your time and an excellent [or very informative] interview on [Monday]. It was a pleasure meeting you and I was most impressed by the high professional standards demonstrated by your staff.

I am certain my [Sales, Marketing or Management] skills would prove extremely valuable as a member of your Northwestern Regional Sales Team. Your product line is excellent, and your company has proven its ability to reach both new and expanding markets.

Once again, thank you for your consideration and I look forward to new career challenges with your excellent firm.

Sincerely,

Susan Winter

ALICE HIKER
1212 Elsewhere Street
Outahere, IL 38281
708/555-2837

RESIGNATION LETTER

Mr. Past Boss
Current Company
1818 Awkward Street
Pension, IL 38281

Dear Mr. Boss:

A new career [or job] opportunity has become available, and I feel it is time to move on to new challenges. Therefore, please consider this my letter of resignation.

Thank you for the opportunity to be a part of this company [or organization]. I wish you and everyone at Current Company continued success in your endeavors. [Optional: Feel free to contact me if you require assistance with work in which I was involved.]

[OR you could begin this letter with:]

My position with Current Company has been rewarding; however, a new career [or job] opportunity has become available, and I feel it must be pursued. Therefore, I am submitting this letter as my formal resignation.

Once again, thank you for letting me be a part of Current Company.

Sincerely yours,

Alice Hiker

REFERENCE SHEET EXAMPLE

PETER NICHOLSON

REFERENCES

Business:

Willie Faul
SureWet Boats, Inc.
739 Stream Highway
Lombard, OH 15014
513/555-0825

Bob Bradford, Partner
Arthur Andersen
250 South Wacker Drive
Chicago, IL 60606
312/555-1800

Daniel Burke, VP Sales/Marketing
Bluebird, Inc.
P.O. Box 460
SouthRidge, IN 46540
219/555-5861

Edward Blade, President
Blade Sales, Inc.
1008 Brady Avenue N.W.
Atlanta, GA 30318
404/555-1133

Personal:

Betty Spin, Marketing Manager
Honda Corporation
P.O. Box 1231
Barrington, IL 60011
708/555-4446

Bobbie Redson, Sales Manager
Perfect Photo Engraving
1112 South Prairie Avenue
Chicago, IL 60616
708/555-9119

Steve Daniels, CPA
Beach Accounting & Tax Service
1162 South Rt. 41
Willowbrook, IL 60514
708/555-8800

William Gates
S&L Leasing Associates
1221 South Cook Road
Northbrook, IL 60062
708/555-5353

SALARY HISTORY EXAMPLE

PETER NICHOLSON

Salary History

(Annual Basis)

StaffLink, Inc.
Human Resources Representative $28,000

DeskTop Publishing, Inc.
Staff Writer   Up to $24,000: Commission Based

Union Van Lines
Corporate Recruiter $25,000

Enron Natural Gas, Inc.
Writer and Branch Manager   Up to $30,000: Commission Based

Notes:

* You could also add: Current salary requirements are open to negotiation.

* If salary requirements are requested, you could add:
  Currently seeking a position in the low $30s ($40s, etc.) per year.

  Remember that this could label you as overpriced or underpriced for the position.
  That's one reason they ask for a salary history in the first place.
  Also remember that unless you feel it's essential, include salary history and/or requirements only when requested by the employer.

Chapter 9

Broadcast Letters

Some people swear by them, others swear at them. They're called Broadcast or Personal Sales letters, and in some cases they can effectively replace a resume and help you get an interview. The Broadcast letter relieves the hiring authority from the "just another resume" mentality and offers a viable alternative. Here you emphasize only knowledge and experience directly applicable to the position at hand.

Broadcast letters are best used when no position has been advertised and you're looking to spark interest in your qualifications with an executive, manager or whomever is the hiring authority. I recommend them only to those seeking executive-level or managerial positions that may or may not already exist at a particular organization. They must be sent directly to the person who would appreciate and possibly hire someone with your qualifications.

GENERAL FORMAT

Begin the text of your letter with the most impressive, unique aspects of your career. You must immediately grasp the attention of this busy executive and entice him or her to take a minute to get to know you. After all, they haven't requested any resumes or applications, so why should they read yours?

Start with a brief summary of where you are now and what you have accomplished with your current or most recent employer. In these attention-getting paragraphs, capitalize your position title(s):

- As Chief Design Engineer with Compu-Best, I managed a staff of six and was solely responsible for acquiring this firm's largest overseas account.

OR:

- As Senior Financial Officer for a big-eight accounting firm, my efforts have streamlined collection procedures and reduced delinquent accounts by 12 percent.
- As Director of Marketing for General Motor's appliance division, I planned and implemented marketing strategies that increased refrigerator sales 21 percent in FY 1989. (Notice in the above example that you don't detail exactly how you accomplished the sales increase; the reader will have to call you in to find out. Also, using *FY* rather than *fiscal year* shows a certain respect to both your own and the reader's experience in senior-level management.)
- I speak five languages fluently, have traveled extensively and acquired profitable accounts in Europe and Japan. Throughout my career, I've been instrumental in long- and short-term budget planning, resulting in the successful penetration of markets previously considered inaccessible.

What languages, what specific markets, in what countries? Don't tell them in this letter. Here's where you generate curiosity and make them want to meet such an achiever. Just don't let your wording sound cocky or you may be perceived as a snob.

In the introductory paragraph, you don't need to list your current employer, which ensures confidentiality. Although this is an advantage over most Functional resumes, remember that you still must include your name, and if your industry is small and close-knit, your current employer may hear that you're looking for a new position. However, this is unlikely and most employers will respect your privacy.

In the final paragraph, tell the reader when you will be available for an interview and request that they contact you as soon as possible to arrange a meeting. Whenever possible, however, you should take the initiative and call the employer to set an interview:

I will be calling you within one week to arrange a personal interview. Meanwhile, please feel free to contact me for any further information you may require.

OR:

I will be in Boston September 5th through the 10th and can be reached at the Sheraton Hotel downtown, 212/555-8847. I look forward to discussing mutual interests.

Sincerely,

Ronald E. Jones

Following are two examples of broadcast letters.

MICHAEL T. SMITH   *BROADCAST LETTER*
576 Cherry Street
Broadview, CA 12789
609/555-1736

Mr. James Williamson, President
Armstrong Associates
518 College Avenue
DeKalb, IL 60115

Dear Mr. Williamson:

As Director of Life Insurance Sales for a Fortune 500 firm, I have been successful in directing a sales force of 1,250 while creating and implementing innovative marketing strategies. One such strategy resulted in a 14 percent sales increase in the first quarter of FY 1988.

In view of the phenomenal growth your firm has experienced in group health sales, I would like to present a synopsis of my qualifications in application for a position in Life Insurance Marketing with Armstrong Associates. Throughout my career I have:

- Created marketing concepts that increased sales in low-income territories by 12 percent in the third quarter of FY 1989.

- Designed and written a comprehensive sales training manual, detailing product benefits and in-home sales strategies for clients at various income levels.

- Reduced sales staff turnover by 5 percent in FY 1989 through more effective interface with key personnel and recruitment staff.

- Updated descriptions of sales positions and increased worker output while lowering base salaries.

My experience is augmented with an MBA from the University of Chicago, and I am conducting a night course in Marketing at this institution.

I would appreciate the opportunity to meet with you personally to discuss how my experience may benefit your firm, and will be contacting you soon to arrange an interview. Meanwhile, please let me know if there is any further information you require. I can be reached at the above phone number after 7:00 PM weekdays. Thank you for your time and consideration.

Sincerely,

Michael T. Smith

JOHNATHAN J. PING
2381 West Taylor Street
Chicago, IL 60622
312/555-2872

Human Resources
Graphic Creations
392 Albert Avenue
Elk Grove Village, IL 60202

Dear Hiring Authority:

Having researched several major companies in the printing industry, your company stands out as one of the finest in overall services, annual revenues and potential for market expansion. Therefore, I am sending you this letter outlining my experience in our industry and would like to be considered as part of your team of professionals.

My background includes extensive experience in instrumental analysis and I have published six papers, two of which are based on NMR researches, two on GC, one on EPR and one on X-ray. I consider myself qualified for both routine instrument analysis and R&D activities at your company. Achievements have included:

▸ Employment as MS research chemist for two years with Dow Chemical, where I developed and managed successful NMR research projects, including technical staff recruitment and supervision.

▸ Recognition as Employee of the Year at Dow for creativity, self-motivation and team leadership under strict deadlines and customer demands.

▸ Masters and Bachelors degrees in Chemistry from the University of Science and Technology in China.

Rather than attempt to outline my full range of skills and experience in this short letter, I would welcome the opportunity to speak with you via telephone or during a personal interview. I can provide excellent references upon request, and/or a portfolio of articles and status reports on nonconfidential projects.

Please let me know if there is any further information you require, or if you would like to arrange a meeting. Thank you for your time and consideration.

Sincerely,

Johnathan J. Ping

Chapter 10

Using Your Resume Effectively

At last the writing is finished, you've had it laser typeset, copied or printed and it looks perfect. Most importantly, it reads well—with authority and impact. It does not oversell or undersell your qualifications and uses direct, nononsense, easy to understand language. So what's the next step?

Before you do anything, you must begin your research. Finding a job is a job in itself and you should treat it as such. As mentioned earlier, you can call companies directly for key information. Start reviewing brochures, annual reports, articles and summaries of companies in resource books at your local library, many of which are listed in the back of this book.

Generally, applicants who show a real knowledge of a company stand a much better chance of being hired, or at least interviewed, by that company. Use key facts about a company's market, product lines and current condition in your cover letter. Even if this amounts to one or two lines, it helps differentiate you from applicants who seem to blanket the world with their resume. Of course, research isn't possible with some blind ads. But if you have the time, write a letter emphasizing items in the advertisement.

With this targeted approach, try to send at least 30 resumes per week. Send out all the nontargeted resumes you want, but remember they will most likely be less effective.

EIGHT WAYS TO USE A RESUME TO OPEN DOORS

Resumes are most commonly used to respond to advertisements, but of course, they can be used in many other ways, such as:

1. *Networking.* This is the best way to get a job: through someone you know (or through someone you just know about). Contact as many friends, family members, chamber of commerce acquaintances and especially business leaders as you can to discuss your situation. Do not, however,

begin a conversation with "I'm out of work, can you help me?" Instead, begin talking about their situation and their industry and slowly demonstrate your knowledge, skills and abilities; *then* you can mention that you're currently in transition. There are books written on this topic alone and some are mentioned at the end of this guide. If you are still employed, be sure to maintain confidentiality and offer your resume only to people you really trust. Give copies to your family and friends, or anyone at all you think might know a company president, manager, supervisor or influential professional in your field.

2. *Employment Agencies and Headhunters.* Employment agencies can be quite valuable, or just a waste of time. It's important to note that such firms are paid by their clients to fill specific positions and are not in business to get *you* a job. Employment agencies and placement professionals often have positions that are not advertised due to the client firm's desire for confidentiality or detachment from the screening process. Call the service first to see if they ever have positions similar to what you're looking for. If so, you may wish to fax or mail your resume first, then call them again to see if they need more information or an interview. Register with the more established firms and avoid operations that make promises they can't keep. Refuse to pay resume writing or clerical charges disguised as out-of-pocket expenses. Unless you really believe the agency can help you out, let the employer pay the fees. In general, never pay for a job.

3. *Electronic resume networks.* These are databases consisting of hundreds or thousands of resumes, scanned into a computer. Employers can log-on to the system via modem for a fee and access resumes by skill group, profession and/or a job hunter's geographical preference. You may be able to fax or modem your resume to the database, increasing your phone bill but saving postage, printing and time. See Chapter 6 for tips on preparing your resume for a database. Some of these firms are less reliable than others, so check *The National Business Employment Weekly* and/or *A Job Hunter's Guide to Resume Databases* by Stacey Slaughter Miller for firms that will list your resume. You could also take a look at *Electronic Resumes* by Wayne Gonyea and James Gonyea, and *Electronic Resumes for the New Job Market* by Peter D. Weddle.

4. *Cold calling.* If you're feeling energetic, wear your best business suit and visit companies directly. Fill out applications at businesses in your area, but try to research these companies first and leave a resume with your application. Call the hiring authority the next day and speak with someone directly, if possible.

5. *Different types of advertisements.* You can respond to blind box ads if the position seems perfect for you, but don't expect much. These are used by companies that don't want to be identified and they pay extra for the privilege. This keeps their own employees from learning about the

position and confidentiality is maintained. This type of ad also relieves the firm of maintaining their public image by sending the ubiquitous rejection letter. There are other drawbacks: you can't call or research the company, you don't know where it's located and can't personalize a cover letter. Don't forget advertisements in trade journals and magazines related to your field. Keep in mind that the firm placing the blind ad could be your own.

6. *College placement offices.* It can't hurt to send one or two copies of your resume to the placement office at your old school. Even if you haven't seen the place in years, you never know what leads they can generate.

7. *Career/job fairs.* There are free job fairs at colleges and hotels listed in many Sunday newspapers. Begin with the fairs that charge no admission fee and review the list of firms before you attend. These are great places to drop off resumes with many companies and save time, travel and postage. A cover letter is not expected and these fairs offer immediate, mini-interviews.

8. *Be prepared.* Always keep a stack of resumes in your car. You never know when you may meet someone at a business function, industry meeting, or after-hours party who may be able to pass it along to a hiring authority. A 9" × 12" cardboard priority-postage envelope works great.

Here's a sheet we give to our customers:

TEN STRATEGIES FOR PLANNING AND EXECUTING THE JOB HUNT

1. *Write/get a professional resume and solid base of operations.* When your resume is perfect, consult books on interviewing and get access to an answerphone, computer, laser printer and fax machine for custom cover letters.

2. *Develop a* big world *concept.* Enhance your peripheral vision. Look at any and every opportunity to get your foot in the door. If you're going after a select few companies and agencies, you face tremendous competition. Broaden your search and *network, network, network.*

3. *Target your audience.* Make your target group as large as possible, but remember the 80/20 rule: focus most of your efforts on the 20 percent of your target group of greatest interest. Customize/personalize correspondence and, when possible, tailor your resume to the job.

4. *Be strategic.* Create a marketing plan for your job hunt. You're the product. Share the plan with those you meet. Refine the plan as you go along.

5. *Adjust your search to the market.* Concentrate your search on high-growth markets. Make yourself available for freelance or contract work.

6. *Don't be afraid to phone first.* Be assertive, yet considerate of other's time. Persistence pays. Your goal is to get your name in the employer's head

and/or extract information or even an information interview. Thrive on rejection. Stay positive no matter what happens. Things change—sometimes quickly.

7. *Develop outside interests, but put in regular hours for your search.* If your life is well balanced, finding that next position is less stressful. You'll need endurance. Eat smart, get your sleep and get plenty of exercise.

8. *Be realistic.* In today's economy, it can take up to one month for every $10,000 in salary to find a job. Be prepared to start at a lower paying position if required to supplement your income.

9. *Get attention.* Expand your network by joining a chamber of commerce or professional groups in your industry. Attend luncheons, seminars, dinners and after-hour meetings when possible. Meet new people and develop a network of contacts.

10. *Enjoy the hunt.* Job hunting can be a complex, challenging game with great payoffs for those with drive and stamina. Finding a job is probably the toughest job you'll ever have and you don't even get paid for it, but you will become stronger for the experience.

RESOURCE MATERIALS

The books below can help with your job search. For executives, I recommend *Rites of Passage at $100,000+* by John Lucht. Even if you're not in the $100,000 job range, this book is an excellent guide to job changing. Not a resume guide, it covers the recruitment business and how to make it work for you, personal and nonpersonal networking, direct mailings, interviewing and more.

Visit your local library and ask about these books and other industry references and directories. Also ask about listings and reference materials specific to your industry: advertising, engineering, etc.

Gonyea, Wayne and Gonyea, James. *Electronic Resumes.* New York: McGraw Hill, 1995.

Jud, Brian. *Job Search 101.* Avon, CT: Marketing Directions, Inc., 1991.

Lucht, John. *Rights of Passage at $100,000+.* New York: Holt & Co., 1993.

Provenzano, Steven and The PLA / Public Library Association. *The Guide to Basic Cover Letter Writing.* Lincolnwood, IL: VGM Career Horizons, 1995.

Spina, Vicki. *Getting Hired in the '90s.* Chicago: Dearborn Financial Publishing, 1995.

Weddle, Peter D. *Electronic Resumes for the New Job Market.* San Luis Obispo, CA: Impact Publishing, 1994.

Chapter 11

The Secrets of a Great Interview

Statistically, if you are called in for one interview for every 20 resumes sent to advertisements, you're getting good results. Even if you have several interviews booked, don't get too comfortable. What if an interview gets canceled? You should never stop the process of researching, identifying opportunities and quickly responding to them by phone, fax or mail.

Don't book too many interviews on the same day. Some may run longer than planned and you could be late for your next interview. Never be late for an interview! Leave early and allow for bad weather or traffic jams. Besides, when you book too many interviews in one day, you may find yourself thinking: "Just what does this company do again?" You must always be fresh, alert and able to promptly answer tough questions. The single most important thing to remember about the interview is:

Don't Be Nervous!

Try to stay calm, relaxed and focused. It may be hard to believe, but an interview is not a life or death situation. Relax and just be yourself. Easier said than done? Remember that although you may not be the only candidate being interviewed, when you project calm, poised confidence, you may be the most memorable, and that's often the person who gets hired.

The employer may be interviewing other candidates who come across more relaxed and confident, but don't have the skills and experience you have. Don't let them get the job!

☞ *Tipster...*

An article in the *Chicago Tribune* noted an Accountemps survey. The firm polled 200 executives and found that job seekers who interview in the morning may be viewed more favorably than those with interviews later in the day. About 83 percent of those responding to

the poll said they preferred to interview candidates in the morning. In general, the hiring authorities said they dislike interviewing near times when they usually take a break, so consider scheduling your interview during the most favorable times. Here's a listing of responses:

- **14 percent preferred 9** AM
- **69 percent said 9 – 11** AM
- **1 percent said 11** AM **– 1** PM
- **2 percent said 1 – 3** PM
- **2 percent said 3 – 5** PM
- **2 percent said after 5** PM
- **10 percent said "other"**

The best interviewers can put you at ease right from the start with some light conversation. Unfortunately, some interviewers like to put you on the spot. They actually enjoy intimidating candidates with tough questions or hypothetical situations to see how you react under pressure. It's all part of their process to discover what you're made of.

Keep your cool and focus on answering the question to the best of your ability. Thoughtfully consider your replies and maintain eye contact. I recommend reading Vicki Spina's *Getting Hired in the '90s* before any interviewing.

☞ *Tipster . . .*

KEEP ON SMILING

According to a recent survey by Robert Half and Accountemps recruiters, a full 60 percent of executives from the nation's largest companies said they consider their administrative assistants' opinions of applicants to be an important part of the selection process. The survey found that "the interview begins from the moment you start speaking with the executive's assistant."

Assistants are seen as being increasingly skilled at gauging whether candidates will be a good fit for the company's business environment and executives take this into account when making hiring decisions. Some assistants actually interview candidates, either formally if they also serve as office managers, or informally as a means of facilitating the screening process.

If you can go into an interview with a relaxed, yet confident attitude, you may be able to tame the most intimidating interviewer. It helps to remember that he or she probably sat right where you are and answered the same questions to get the job. You will still be asked the tough questions, but your conversation can become a more informative, meaningful and natural dialogue. After interviewing hundreds of job applicants, I found the more relaxed the candidate became, the more relaxed I also became. I still asked the tough questions I always did, but our conversation was much more informative and natural.

Get excited about the interview as a discovery process, as one more step on the road to your successful career. Imagine that you're going to meet and converse with one of your future colleagues. Answer questions completely but be succinct, and feel free to ask questions about the company without appearing skeptical.

Give the interviewer an honest impression of confidence without being boisterous, personality without excess and intelligence without a know-it-all attitude.

If you remain calm and measured in your answers and the interviewer seems inattentive, overbearing, or gives vague responses to questions about compensation, work hours or specific job duties, this may not be the best company for you. Perhaps you should find a better place to spend 40 or more hours every week.

Throughout the entire job search process, always keep a positive attitude and no matter what happens act professional and courteous with the receptionist and everyone you meet. They may be your future colleagues. And lest we forget, dress like a professional. When you keep a winning attitude, others will notice you and want you to be a part of their world. Remember that certain job skills can always be taught, but it's much harder to teach a person how to get along with clients or coworkers.

Everyone wants to be around a winner, so act like a winner.

CHAPTER 12

Top Secret Resume Examples

All of the following resumes were produced on a personal computer and laser printer. The first 12 of these resumes are annotated, with numbers corresponding to the notes below.

This is a sampling of resumes I've written over the years for my clients. The first two use none of the extra design features offered by computers, such as small boxes (instead of bullets), bold facing, italics or proportional type fonts. This demonstrates the type of resume you could produce using a regular typewriter.

Just about all the other examples are laser typeset in CG (Courier Gothic), Times or Helvetica, at between 11 and 12 points. Some of the two-page resumes are printed on the front and back of a single sheet, but you should never do this with your resume.

Take the time to scan as many resumes as you can that match—or are related to—your industry. Make a list of the best wordings and ideas from all these samples to create your own self-marketing tool. I've tried to include a good cross-section of resumes from different fields, and there are many different ways to write about your most applicable talents. These methods may at first seem to conflict, but they are simply different, effective ways of writing about your skills, work experience and education.

NOTES ON RESUME EXAMPLES

1. These examples use both *percent* and % to show how each appears. *Percent* is recommend in the Associated Press Stylebook. The % sign is of course much shorter and used more often in daily correspondence. I therefore recommend % for your resume, though both are certainly acceptable.

2. Many of the resume examples that follow have margins smaller than one inch. I did this to add as much information as possible for use on your own resume, but you should always use 3/4" to 1" of white space on all sides of your resume text.

These notes correspond to the numbers in parentheses in the resumes on pages 90–105:

Catherine N. Myers

(1) Here is a short summary of the most common and important office activities and the equipment used to complete them. The second bullet covers people skills: training, supervision and communications. (2) We began with Catherine's last position because it was most relevant. The Objective is Office Management, and using reverse chronological places this supervisory position at the top to grab attention. Also, company name is placed above job titles, so that "Blue Shirt Warehouse" company below acts as the umbrella above various positions. (3) Turns ordinary pack & ship work into an important, high-volume operation. (4) Listing all positions shows a progression through the company. The highest position obtained, Administrative Assistant, lasted only one month before termination, so I omitted dates for each position. (5) Writing "Successful completion of. . ." helps cover for lack of college degree.

Gregory Henson

(1) Demonstrates analytical skills and a knowledge of where to find and utilize information on businesses, a key talent in both product and service businesses. (2) Shows a knowledge of computer systems and their application to banking functions. (3) Listing all three titles gives a picture of advancement based on performance.

Randall Kraft

(1) Here's an Objective targeted not only by profession, but to specific types of products. Change "food service industry" to your field: electronics, software, switches, office equipment, etc. (2) A summary of all general areas throughout the years; the next three bullets are applicable to almost every major sales position. Pick the ones that apply to you and others pertaining to your goals. Randall had an M.B.A., and knew this was required for some positions he was seeking, so I mentioned it again here; otherwise, avoid mentioning college degrees in your summary. (3) Dollar volumes under Marketing verify Randall's talents and give them power. If confidentiality is a major concern, omit company names and use only titles, but most readers respect your privacy. Dates are optional if you wish to omit jobs, but can raise questions; best to include if you're not compromised.

John Walters

(1) I kept John's Objective and Experience short to make enough room for hands-on employment for a position in Retail. (2) Shows a willingness to work long hours, a virtual necessity in retail environments. (3) Backs up "profitability" under Experience. (4) Spanish can be very useful in retail, especially with stockers and warehouse personnel. "Excellent communication skills" is optional, but here it helps fill out the page, as does the layout of college course titles.

Steven A. Provolone

(1) No Objective here, but it is implied with summary of "More than four years in. . ." Steven was emphasizing his experience in candidate interviewing and human resources. I made it a combination format and highlighted his experience in personnel, while downplaying his editing and writing background. (2) Shows ability to use previous writing experience in conjunction with recruiting. (3) "Temporary" explains brevity of the position. (4) Emphasis on developing job descriptions; explains brevity of position. (5) Name dropping of publications, with most important first, in this case the *National Business Employment Weekly.*

Gary L. Larson

This college graduate received four interviews and four job offers after mailing 20 laser prints of this resume. (1) We used only a title since Gary, like many college graduates, had no specific job objective. We gave the reader a general area for which he could be considered. (2) The key to the success of this resume is in the Experience section. Here I took skills developed in part-time employment and college activities (including course work and fraternity functions) and wrote about them in business-oriented language. The second bullet is derived from speech classes and coordination of activities for different groups. The third bullet comes from different part-time jobs.

Maxwell Borden

(1) If you're a new college graduate, the best way to distance yourself from the pack is to include jargon of the field you've studied. This demonstrates a general knowledge of the industry and gives the impression you have a business-like mentality. (2) A good way to fill the page is to list your most relevant courses, and, even more importantly, any major term papers or research you completed. Did you do any research of local businesses and their practices? How did your course work prepare you for the real business world? Explain it here. (3) This Personal section helps fill the page and balance the stereotype of accountants as number crunchers.

Wilma Ferguson

(1) A specific Objective for a specific goal. Experience outlines total years of experience under various titles, and touches on types of subjects taught. (2) A short description because school leaders know her already. (3) Lists degree but more important, shows continuation of education after college to keep up with trends in PC instruction and teaching of exceptional (LD) students. (4) Shows training in Spanish; although we intentionally omit that this was mostly during her high school years, it's important to include for a position at a language academy. This section also shows a strong interest in volunteer work and after-hours input. Additional note: dates omitted from Prior Experience because this was 14 years ago, so "One Year" is preferred.

Gerald Cartwright

(1) This is a great way to get attention and create an air of knowledgeability, and always be honest! Never lie on your resume because someday you will have to back it up. (2) Communication skills are important in any position, but especially in management. The ability to work with unions is essential at some companies. (3) Avoid total time with the firm in this case to conceal your age, then list specific dates at various positions. (4) LIFO/FIFO stands for last in/first out and first in/first out. Using the abbreviated form shows experience and projects Gerald at his proper level of expertise. (5) Important to show size of an otherwise unknown firm. (6) Shows initiative and leadership, as well as motivation to work himself through college by listing "100 percent of college costs." (7) Helps fill the page and could be deleted to save space.

Berry Orange

(1) This Objective can certainly be deleted if it's too limiting or if space is at a premium. Remember that specific objectives can always be stated in the cover letter once you've determined the needs and specialties of individual firms. (2) Due to lack of an Experience section and the complexity of legal work, this job description should be fairly well detailed. But don't tell your readers everything about your position, just enough to leave them wanting to learn more about you and how you've accomplished these goals. (3) Don't elaborate on something as simple as this position, just let them know the experience was worthwhile and helped pay for college. (4) Make this the umbrella above multiple degrees when possible and you avoid listing 1975 three times. Adds readability and reduces fatigue.

Debra Roberts

(1) Account acquisition is perhaps the most valuable sales skill, and the ability to manage those accounts is a close second. (2) "High-energy sales" is

unique and therefore gets attention. (3) Used to show reason for accepting temporary work rather than sales, which she was having trouble finding upon relocation. (4) Numbers are always valuable in Sales resumes, but don't overuse! (5) Downplay company ownership; some managers may think you have trouble taking orders or will use their methods to start your own firm. (6) Long ago, so dates are omitted.

Robin Sings

(1) With the huge and sometimes confusing variety of computer positions, keep your Objective as specific as possible and change as needed. Remember they may be hiring for several computer-oriented positions simultaneously. (2) Experience section here is optional, especially if you have more hardware, software or languages to list on the page. If such is the case, don't let Experience push you into two pages. (3) This is the most important section, with previous positions and employers running a very close second. You can use qualifiers such as "fluent in" (languages), "familiar with," "proficient in" or "experience in." (4) Don't mention every project with your previous employers, just the most important ones with impressive clients such as NASA. Do try to touch on communication, presentation and client-relation skills whenever possible in order to stand above those who have only worked with bits and bytes. As in any field, remember that employers may require confidentiality about certain systems, designs and products. Be careful what you tell the competition.

COMBINATION/CHRONOLOGICAL
(Numbers explained on pg. 86)

CATHERINE N. MYERS

287 Lewis Drive	Salem, OR 67488	723/555-1730

OBJECTIVE:

ADMINISTRATIVE SUPPORT / OFFICE MANAGEMENT
A position where proven organizational skills would be utilized.

PROFILE:

- Experience in basic accounting including billing, inventory control and order entry on IBM and WANG systems; familiar with Lotus 1-2-3, WordPerfect 5.1 and WordStar.

(1)

- Assist in staff hiring, training and supervision with solid communication skills; handle customer complaints and problems with tact and professionalism.

EMPLOYMENT:

Alomo Canyon Hotel, Bloomingdale, VA   1980-1987
ASSISTANT SUPERVISOR

(2)

Responsible for training and supervising one assistant in order entry and billing for this high-volume resort with ski lodge, restaurant and hotel.
Worked directly with the clientele: booked reservations, distributed keys and delivered phone messages in the absence of regular front desk staff.
* Promoted to this position from Front Desk Clerk.
* Volume of positive customer response cards increased by 20 percent in the last two months at this position.

Speedy-Quick Shop, Richmond, VA   1987-1988
ORDER ENTRY ASSISTANT
Utilized an IBM PC for order expediting and the printing of customer invoices.

(3)

Packed and shipped hundreds of individual orders via the post office, UPS and various overnight carriers.

Blue Shirt Warehouse, Newton, VA   1988-Present
Promoted to three positions, most recent first:
ADMINISTRATIVE ASSISTANT
Responsible for order entry, stock transfers and price code updates on a Wang terminal.
Work directly with store managers to facilitate new openings.
Expedite stock procurement and the delivery of store fixtures.

MERCHANDISING REPRESENTATIVE
Acted as liaison between managers of six stores and corporate directors.

WAREHOUSE REPRESENTATIVE

(4)

Distributed bulk shipments to 54 stores nationwide.

EDUCATION:

Oakton Community College, Richmond, VA   5/88

(5)

Successful completion of courses in English, Algebra and Psychology.

GREGORY J. HENSON

232 Winter Line Road
Pittsburgh, PA 60948
708/555-9814

PROFILE:

- More than 12 years in finance, including full P&L responsibility for commercial credit lines at a major bank with over $40 million in assets.

- Effectively hire, train and supervise loan officers and support personnel in product introduction and the professional management of key accounts.

EMPLOYMENT:

Cold-Taylor Bank, Pittsburgh, PA   1985-Present
DIRECTOR, COMMERCIAL FINANCE   1987-Present
In charge of developing and marketing commercial credit lines to small and medium-sized firms in the northwestern suburbs.

(1) Analyze local industry trends and determine/meet client's specific business needs.
Negotiate contracts with company principals and officers.
- Volume of new loans increased 21 percent, 1989.
- Volume of new loans increased 18 percent, 1989.
- Manage two supervisors and a staff of ten.

(2) - Assisted in the procurement and implementation of new computer hardware and software to speed computation and delivery of amortization schedules, resulting in greater client satisfaction as reflected in postsale surveys.

LOAN OFFICER   1985-1987
Responsible for loan origination and processing, including negotiations and the scheduling of capital assessments.
- Assisted in orienting new loan officers in account management and computer system operation.

Hoffman Bank, Pittsburgh, PA   1981-1985
LOAN OFFICER   1983-1985

(3) Gained excellent experience in loan origination and client relations.
- Trained two employees in bank loan procedures and computer systems.

PERSONAL FINANCE COUNSELOR   1983-1985
Counseled individuals and assisted in meeting their long- and short-term business goals.

TELLER   1981-1983

EDUCATION:

Utah University, Gnome, UT   Graduated Cum Laude, 1981
B.A. Degree, Finance/Administration   Minor: Economics
* Elected President of the Finance and Banking Club.

RANDALL KRAFT

2111 Kalzone Drive
Bartlett, IL 60987

FUNCTIONAL
(Numbers explained on page 86)

708/555-7654

OBJECTIVE:

(1)

A position utilizing extensive experience in Sales or Sales Management, preferably in the sale of equipment and supplies to the food service industry.

EXPERIENCE:

(2)

- More than 15 years in food service, including full responsibility for equipment sales, restaurant management and the setup and operation of new locations; M.B.A. Degree, DePaul University.

- Experience in budget planning and sales forecasting, as well as market research and new product introduction.

- Plan and conduct sales presentations in a professional manner; design and utilize sales support materials including videotapes, brochures and detailed user guides.

- Skilled in executive-level contract negotiations; utilize CAD systems and SmartCom to develop equipment configurations and meet specific client needs.

- Effectively hire, train and supervise sales personnel; interface with senior-level executives in the planning and implementation of sales incentive programs.

MAJOR ACHIEVEMENTS:

(3)

Management
Reduced turnover of Sales Representatives 22 percent at most recent position by improving training programs and compensation structures. Hired and trained an inside sales force of 21, exceeding all previous annual sales records in the Midwest for a leading food service firm.

Administration
Provided full interface between accounting and executive personnel in the design of a computerized order entry and billing system.
Reduced delinquent accounts by 19 percent.

Marketing
Conducted in-depth regional market research and acquired exclusive rights to supply ovens, freezers and dishwasher equipment to a rapidly expanding chain of pizza stores. Sales exceeded $1 million, first six months. Projected sales for 1991: $4 million.

EMPLOYMENT:

So-Cool Products, Washington, DC   **Sales Manager** 1983-Present

Litton Corporation, Los Angeles, CA   **Sales Representative** 1980-1983

EDUCATION:

DePaul University, Chicago, IL
M.B.A. Degree   1977

JOHN WALTERS

COMBINATION

123 Smoke Street
Oasis, CA 60987

(Numbers explained on pg. 87)
710/555-8154

OBJECTIVE:

Retail Sales Management
A position where profit-building skills would be utilized.

EXPERIENCE:

- More than 12 years in retail sales management, including full responsibility for staffing, inventory control and effective customer service.

(1)

EMPLOYMENT:

Assistant Manager   9/83-6/89
Target Corporation, Oasis, CA
Effectively hired, trained and supervised up to 21 employees in direct customer service, sales and store maintenance/security.
In charge of budget planning and forecasting, as well as sales reporting and cost-effective stock procurement.
* Utilized an NCR SAT/EPOS system for the storing and modification of data related to advertisements.

(2)

* Maintained accuracy of invoicing and billing; managed shipping/receiving and worked with home office staff.
* Occasionally worked nights during 24-hour grand openings.

(3)

* Profits increased 15% to $640,000 on sales of $7.5 million.

Manager   9/73-9/83
K-Mart Corporation, various Chicagoland locations
In charge of 14 employees and all lunch counter operations.
Managed stock ordering, inventory control and retail display setup.
Responsible for all sales, advertising coordination and office administration.
Communicated with vendors, suppliers and customers in a professional manner.
* Profits increased 30% on sales of $600,000 annually.

EDUCATION:

W.R. Harper College, Palatine, IL   1975-1977

Successful completion of courses in:
- Business Management   - Sociology
- English   - Biology

* Achieved ACT score of 26; Overall GPA: 3.4/4.0

Logan High School, Chicago, IL   1975
* Earned State Scholarship

(4)

PERSONAL:

Conversant in Spanish; self-motivated, with communication and organizational skills applicable to new business environments.

STEVEN A. PROVOLONE   *(Numbers explained on pg. 87)* COMBINATION

221 Drivers Lane
Streamwood, AL 60687   **232/555-2524**

EXPERIENCE: ‣   More than three years in staff interviewing and recruiting, including hands-on experience in virtually all aspects of corporate human resources.

(1)   ‣   Skilled in designing forms for employee tracking and timely performance review; document disciplinary and counseling methods; work directly with trainers, staff and management in employee orientation, promotion and motivation.

EMPLOYMENT: Stafflink, Inc., Roselle, IL   6/89-Present
                 Corporate Recruiter / HR Representative
                 Responsible for recruiting and personnel activities for 72 employees at this research firm. This is the largest firm in the world specializing in the compilation and sale of reports outlining qualifications of professionals in primarily high-tech fields.
                 Duties include employee counseling and file updating; utilize WordPerfect and AREV software to track performance reviews and departmental succession plans.
                 Write/place advertisements and post jobs at numerous colleges and no-cost services. Monitor ad response and cost per hire.

(2)   -   Conducted more than 180 interviews.
                 -   Conducted research and wrote/distributed a concise biography of this company for free inclusion in such publications as What Color Is Your Parachute?, The Macmillan Directory of Leading Private Companies, How To Get A Job In Chicago and The Chicago Job Bank.
                 -   Created and implemented seven new forms related to worker status and applicant interviewing.
                 -   Commended by the Research Analyst Supervisor for reducing turnover 18 percent in the first three months.

                 Chainlink Employment, Inc., Schaumburg, IL   9/88-6/89
                 Staff Writer
                 Created this temporary position for myself.
(3)   Wrote resumes and job search materials on a referral basis for Anderson clientele, providing an excellent opportunity to learn employment agency operations and recruitment methods.

                 -   Recognized by company president for producing virtually capital-free revenues.

                 Allied Van Lines, Oak View, IL   2/88-9/88
                 Corporate Recruiter
                 Accepted this six-month position to assist in recruiting and the relocation of
(4)   National's corporate headquarters from Green Brook to Oak View.

                 -   Recognized by Operations Management for providing more than 50 qualified candidates for Service Representative and Fleet Coordinator positions, most of whom were hired.

<u>Unclear News,</u> Des Plaines, IL   2/87-2/88
Assistant Editor
Solely responsible for final editing and proofreading of this newspaper which runs up
to 42 pages and provides in-depth coverage of energy issues for legislators and
business leaders worldwide.
- Researched and wrote a column entitled People In The News.
- Trained/supervised production staff and acted as liaison between writers and
  editors of the paper and all camera staff and printers.
- Selected and sized photographs, edited copy and assisted in layout; operated a
  dedicated MYCRO-TEK word processor and photo typesetter.

<u>Flashy Career Consultants,</u> Chicago, IL   2/84-2/87
Writer and Branch Manager
Conducted comprehensive interviews with thousands of professionals and executives.
Wrote detailed job descriptions and worker profiles, up to four pages in length, for
purposes of career placement.

- In charge of all operations at three offices; achieved highest production volume
  of five locations.
- Achieved 99 percent client satisfaction through concise writing and effective
  customer service.

EDUCATION: **Bachelor of Arts Degree**   5/83
                        Major: Journalism - Public Relations Emphasis
(5)   <u>Southern Illinois University,</u> Carbondale, IL

FREELANCE   Wrote news and feature articles appearing in:
WRITING: <u>The National Business Employment Weekly, The Chicago Tribune, Lerner/Voice</u>
                        <u>Newspapers, Chicago Sounds Magazine, The Illinois Entertainer, The Xerox Centre</u>
                        <u>Newsletter (Chicago Office) and the Public Relations Society of America (PRSA)</u>
                        <u>Newsletter.</u>

GARY L. LARSON

1121 Wicka Lane   *COMBINATION/New College Graduate (Numbers explained on pg. 87)*
Wild Rose, NE 26252   414/555-5892

(1)   ***ADMINISTRATION / MANAGEMENT***

PROFILE: ■   Proven abilities in human relations, staff training and motivation; well versed in
                        group dynamics and processes.

(2)   ■   Plan & conduct written and oral presentations in a professional manner; organize
                        meetings, programs and events.

                    ■   Hands-on experience in vendor relations, customer service and sales; write &
                        distribute correspondence; coordinate budgets and business operations.

EDUCATION: University of Illinois, Urbana-Champaign, IL
                    Bachelor's Degree, Major: Psychology   Graduated 5/93
                    *   Pledge class Social Chairman: Delta Upsilon Fraternity.

                    Elgin Community College, Elgin, IL
                    Activities required extensive human relation, motivation and organizational skills:
                    *   Elected to ECC's College Community Council, representing the student body
                        among various community groups and the general public.
                    *   Represented ECC at various conferences: NACA, ACUI & ICCSAA.
                    *   Served as coordinating Vice President for the Student Senate.
                    *   Co-founder of first Phi Alpha Delta pre-law fraternity at any Junior College.
                    *   Awarded Leadership Scholarship for two consecutive years.
                    *   Served as Chairman of the Clubs and Organizations Committee.
                    *   Attended numerous leadership seminars.

EMPLOYMENT: Land's End, Bloomingdale, IL   11/92-1/93
                    Sales Associate
                    Handled direct customer service, sales and inventory control.
                    *   Ranked #2 in sales of 16 Associates in first month.

                    Super Sealers, Bartlett, IL   Summer, 1991
                    Co-Owner
                    Hired, trained, motivated and supervised four employees.
                    Responsible for marketing, sales promotions and professional customer relations.

                    Rosati's Pizza, Bartlett, IL   Summer, 1991
                    Shift Leader
                    Trained and supervised several employees in sales and all store operations.

                    C.B.G.B., Inc., Chicago, IL   Summers & Breaks, 6/85-8/89
                    Inventory Control Clerk
                    Placed incoming equipment & supplies; assisted in shipping & receiving.
                    Tracked sales and configured a computerized vendor system.

MAXWELL BORDEN

COMBINATION/NEW GRAD.
(Numbers explained on pg. 87)

176 Pistakee Drive
McHenry, TN 68697

515/555-2918

OBJECTIVE:	A position in Accounting, where comprehensive skills and training would be utilized.

PROFILE:

(1)

- Trained in a full range of accounting functions including inventory control, accounts payable/receivable and general ledger maintenance.

- Familiar with Lotus 1-2-3 on the IBM PC, as well as word processing with WordPerfect 5.1 and WordStar.

- Plan and conduct speeches and presentations in a professional manner; reached state semifinal level as Debate Team member.

EDUCATION:

<u>Tennessee University,</u> DeKalb, TN
B.S. Degree   Graduated May, 1990
Major: Accounting; Minor: Economics

Courses included experience in/with:

(2)

- Business Mathematics	- Statistical Process Control
- AP/AR	- Tax Accounting
- Cost Analyses	- Payroll
- Auditing	- Ledger Updating

* President, Accounting Club, 1989. Successfully recruited new members through advertising and aggressive campaigning on campus.
* Overall GPA: 3.4/4.0
* Self-funded 80% of college costs through part-time and Summer employment at:

<u>Prince Albert Dry Cleaning,</u> McHenry, TN   1986-1990
Bookkeeper/Sales Clerk
Assisted in manual bookkeeping at this busy store serving a community of 40,000.
Handled general cash transactions using an electronic register.
Maintained excellent rapport with customers and developed a repeat clientele.

PERSONAL:
(3)

Energetic and self-motivated, with an excellent attention to detail and a high aptitude for figures.
Enjoy skiing, cycling and jogging.
Willing to travel or relocate.

WILMA FERGUSON   *COMBINATION (Numbers explained on pg. 88)*

1145 Salem Lane   **Rolling Knolls, MA 60965**   **201/555-2415**

OBJECTIVE: *ELEMENTARY TEACHER*
(1)   A position utilizing leadership skills and a strong desire to work with and nurture students to achieve their greatest potential.

PROFILE: • More than 14 years in teaching as an instructional aide and full-time substitute, including full responsibility for lesson planning, material selection and performance review.

                    • Utilize Macintosh systems for teaching Mathematics, Social Studies and Computer Science to normal and learning disabled students.

EMPLOYMENT: **Substitute, Full-Time Basis**   1987-Present
                    St. Patrick Language Academy, Boston, MA
(2)   Responsible for teaching intermediate grades in all general subjects.
                    Acted as Cadre Substitute for six months.

                    Instructional Aide - High School Section   1980-1987
                    Northwest Suburban Special Education Organization, Boston, MA
                    Developed lesson plans and evaluated students.
                    Worked directly with the teacher in sourcing appropriate classroom materials and creating new student challenges.

                    * Utilized Apple PCs in a classroom environment for the instruction of Composition, Typing, Social Studies and Mathematics.

                    Teacher   One Year
                    Bryant School and Lloyd School, Massachusetts Board of Education, Boston, MA

EDUCATION: Champaign University, Normal, IL
                    B.S. Degree, Elementary Education

(3)   Chicago Teaching University, Chicago, IL
                    Diagnosis and Remediation of Reading Problems, 1988
                    Personal computer use in the Classroom, 1987; The Exceptional Child, 1986

                    W.R. Harper College, Palatine, IL
(4)   Completed courses in WordPerfect and WordStar, 1987.

PERSONAL: Trained extensively in Spanish; traveled in Spain, France and Italy.
                    Actively support the PTA. Secretary for the PPAC at Bryant School.
                    Seeking to volunteer for the St. Patrick's proposed after school program.

GERALD CARTWRIGHT

2116 Cave Lane
Gotham City, NY 29282

908/555-4320

OBJECTIVE: A Management position utilizing professional talents in the setup and cost-effective management of inventory control and purchasing systems.

PROFILE:

- More than 12 years in purchasing, inventory control and the direction of internal logistics for major warehousing and distribution activities.

(1)

- Skilled in budget planning and sales forecasting, as well as general accounting, bookkeeping and cost analysis/reduction.

- Handle procedure development and system streamlining through comprehensive labor and cost analyses.

- Effectively hire, train and motivate team leaders and supervisors; plan and implement worker incentive programs that have proven to reduce turnover.

(2)

- Plan and conduct speeches and training sessions in a professional manner; act as liaison between union leaders and corporate executives.

EMPLOYMENT: Digger's Clamps, Bensenville, NY
Manager: Inventory Control   1985-Present

(3)   Manage an entire inventory of various distributed and manufactured goods, with stock consistently valued at over $42 million.
In charge of three crew supervisors; indirectly supervise 29 employees in warehousing, purchasing and distribution.

- *   Authorize customer credits, exchanges and all shipments exceeding $675,000.
- *   Expedite delivery dates and generate status reports using Lotus.
- *   Successfully negotiated stock purchase and warehousing contracts with vendors and the clientele.

(4)   *   Initiated LIFO and FIFO programs resulting in faster deliveries worldwide.
- *   Reviewed the entire base of raw product vendors and recommended new vendors as needed, resulting in a savings of $21,000 in FY 1992.

Team Supervisor   1982-1985
Effectively supervised a team of 12 stockers and forklift drivers in order picking, stocking and truck loading/unloading.

- *   Assisted in improving warehouse layout, resulting in faster location of items.

Payne, Johnson, Weber, Bensenville, NY   1976-1982
Supervisor: Shipping and Receiving   1979-1982
Responsible for shipping and receiving functions for this manufacturer of electronic components for the personal electronics industry.

(5)

* Annual sales in 1982: $15 million.
* Operated a Sperry computer terminal in shipment/order tracking.
* Managed a crew of six including forklift drivers, truck drivers and stockers.

Shipping/Receiving Clerk   1976-1979
Gained excellent experience in order entry via telephone; communicated with the clientele on a daily basis.
Performed hand writing of customer invoices prior to assisting in the conversion from manual to computerized operations.

* Voted Employee of the Month five times.
* Recognized by management for loyalty, drive and the ability to work well under pressure, according to annual performance reviews.

**PRIOR
EXPERIENCE:**   Self-funded 90% of college costs through employment at:

(6)   White Castle, Syracuse, NY   1975-1976
Line Manager, Part-Time
Supervised a crew of 16 in customer service, order taking and cooking, in accordance with strict corporate guidelines.

* Promoted to this position from order taker and cook.

Cool Head's Place, Syracuse, NY   1972-1975
Painter
Responsible for direct customer service and custom interior/exterior painting during weekends, holidays and spring & summer breaks.

EDUCATION: Syracuse University, Syracuse, NY
B.A. Degree   Graduated 1976
Major: Business; Minor: Logistic and Inventory Management.

* Graduated Cum Laude
* Dean's List, 1975

(7)

Courses included experience in Basic Computer Operation, Statistics, Advanced Algebra and General Accounting.

BERRY ORANGE

124 East Chestnut #243
Phoenix, AZ 60698
612/555-9876

REVERSE CHRONOLOGICAL
(Numbers explained on pg. 88)

OBJECTIVE:

(1)

A position utilizing an extensive background in Administrative Law.

CAREER BACKGROUND:

(2)

United States Department of Education, Office for Civil Rights, Phoenix, AZ
2/80-Present

Attorney/Advisor
Primarily involved in civil rights compliance determinations, providing advice and analyses for the planning and execution of investigations related to virtually all types of discrimination.

Responsible for tracing funds utilized by various agencies and programs receiving federal assistance.
Negotiate directly with agency officials and interpret/enforce federal guidelines.

- Accept full-charge responsibility for numerous enforcement proceedings.
- Determine jurisdiction for specific cases.
- Review applications for federal funds.
- Assigned as Coordinating Attorney for regional technical assistance related to statutes enforced by the U.S.D.E. office for Civil Rights.

As Law Librarian, effectively manage a 2,000-volume library for
U.S.D.E./O.C.R./C.R.A.S.-v personnel.
- Train colleagues in the use of Westlaw's computerized legal research system.
- Organize quarterly case sessions.
- Monitor activities in bureaus and federal courts on a daily basis for all department attorneys and staff.

Private Law Practice, Miami, FL
1978-1980
Attorney
Responsible for a full range of civil matters, including estates, trusts and wills.
Acted as consultant to Dean of the Miami School of Law in the assessment of public services.

University of Miami School of Law, Miami, FL
1971-1978
Assistant Law Librarian

(3)   Gained an excellent background in the layout and operation of law libraries.
Directly involved in the research of potential new acquisitions.

Law Clerk Experience:

Louis Dartell, Miami, FL   Oct.-Nov. 1978
Flynn, Peters and Havelcheck, Miami, FL   Fall, 1976

EDUCATION: University of Miami School of Law, Miami, FL

J.D., Graduated Cum Laude   1978

- Ranked among the top 20 percent.
- Listed in Who's Who in American Colleges and Universities.
- Dean's List, four semesters.
- Earned Book Award for Civil Procedure I, as well as for Workmen's
  Compensation Certificate of Merit, Student Bar Association.

(4)   Degrees Earned, 1975, each Magna Cum Laude and General Honors:

A.B., Major: Politics and Public Affairs, Minor: History
B.S., Major: Mathematics, Minor: Computer Science
B.G.S., Major: Religion

- National Mock Trial Member, one year.
- Law School Representative on U.M. Health Center Advisory Board.
- U.M. Delegate to O.D.K. National Convention and Province III Convention, two
  consecutive years.
- Board Member and Liaison to U.M. Administration, U.M. Student Government.
- Member, Client Counseling Board, one year.
- Director, Student Bar Book Co-Op.

(Numbers explained on pp. 88–89) **DEBRA ROBERTS** *COMBINATION*

1923 Kitten Lane   Northbrook, OK 60687   228/555-3827

OBJECTIVE:

(1)

INSIDE SALES
A position where proven abilities in account acquisition and management
would be utilized.

EXPERIENCE:

(2)

- More than six years in high-energy sales including full responsibility for cold calling, market penetration and the successful development of major accounts.

- Skilled in staff training and supervision in telephone prospecting, product lines and professional client relations.

EMPLOYMENT:

(3)

Sales / Customer Service   12/89-Present
Salem Temporary Service, Northbrook, OK
A full range of activities include customer service, order taking and telephone sales at two large suburban companies.
Perform data entry/retrieval; utilize Lotus 1-2-3, Windows and WordPerfect.
Accepted these positions upon relocation from Omaha, Nebraska.

Nebraska Sales Representative   1/86-12/89
Jones License and Title Service, Palos Hills, OK
Developed a major Nebraska territory through telephone and in-person cold calling of transportation firms and currency exchanges.
Acquired numerous accounts and maintained solid, profitable relationships with existing accounts in Iowa and Nebraska.
Processed title transactions and administered invoicing, collections and daily bank deposits.

(4)

* Dramatically increased client base from 2 to 96.

Sales Representative   1/86-12/89
Bingo King, Omaha, NE
Responsible for planning and implementing sales concepts and acquiring/ maintaining profitable accounts in a three-state Midwestern region. Products included bingo paper and equipment marketed to mid- and upper-level wholesalers.

* Effectively trained sales representatives in presentations, up-selling and personalized client relations.
* Personally increased monthly sales from $100,000 to $200,000.

Marketing Representative   5/83-12/84
National Econotel, Omaha, NE
Promoted to this position from Inside Sales Representative.

Generated leads via telephone; called on virtually all types of professionals for the sale of long-distance telephone services.
Designed and implemented sales proposals.
Maintained a solid customer base and a high closing ratio.

*   Consistently met or exceeded sales quota of $18,000/month.

(5)   **Owner / Operator**   11/77-4/83
             The Nail Lady, Omaha, NE
             In charge of all sales, marketing and administrative functions at this nail sculpture and electrolysis shop.

             Buyer   5/79-6/82
             Eye On Design, Omaha, NE
             Responsible for customer service, correspondence and the design/purchase of jewelry for a discriminating clientele.

EDUCATION: Moraine Valley Community College, Omaha, NE
                 Nursing Program, completed two years.

                 Accurate College of Hair Removal, Omaha, NE
(6)   Successful completion of a Certification Course.

                 Luther South High School, Omaha, NE
                 Graduate

ROBIN SINGS

1652 South Eastwood Avenue
Seattle, WA 60698
308/555-1832

COMBINATION
(Numbers explained on pg. 89)

OBJECTIVE:

(1)

A **Systems Programming** position utilizing skills applicable to a wide range of hardware and software.

PROFILE:

(2)

► More than six years in systems programming, including the research, writing and development of tractable user procedures and manuals.

► Effectively handle system documentation and full application support at client locations.

Software/Languages:
Proficient in Fortran and COBOL; familiar with BAL, JCL, BASIC, Assembler and Pascal "C." Operating systems include UNIX, OS/MVS and DOS.

(3)

Hardware:
IBM 3033, 370/158, 360/145 and 360/30; Honeywell 437; Univac; Prime 850 and CDC 160-A.

EMPLOYMENT:

(4)

SYSTEMS PROGRAMMER   1987-Present
Microsoft, Inc., Seattle, WA
Act as Team Leader involved in new program design and production for this major supplier of data processing services to NASA.
Installed and maintained OS/MVS on an IBM 360/145.
Trained and supervised software personnel on system modifications.

* Successfully converted UNIX from IBM 3033 to client's Honeywell 437.
* Directly involved in the preparation and submission of a proposal that was accepted by a major automobile manufacturer in Detroit.

SYSTEMS PROGRAMMER   1985-1987
Cyrix Corporation, Seattle, WA
Involved in developing a telecommunications system on Univac and Prime mainframes using BAL, JCL and BASIC.

EDUCATION:

Seattle University, Seattle, WA   Graduated 1985
B.A. Degree: Computer Programming   * Dean's List, 1984

Computer Science courses included training and experience in Operating Systems, Computer Architecture, Data Structures and Discrete Structures.

* Utilized the IBM 3033, 370/158, Honeywell 437 and CDC 160-A.

ALFRED E. JOHNSON
560 Ridge Drive
Bartlett, IL 60313
708/555-7812

COMBINATION

OBJECTIVE: A position with a consulting or engineering firm where experience in nuclear systems maintenance and operations would be utilized.

PROFILE:
- Experienced in reactor plant operations and maintenance; supervise modification & repair work and establish special plant conditions.

- Assist in worker supervision, training and evaluation, as well as work scheduling and training program development/implementation.

EXPERIENCE: *United States Naval Officer*   1985-Present
Nuclear Qualified Surface Warfare Officer
Nuclear Officer Programs Manager, Navy Recruiting District Chicago, Carbondale, IL
9/88-Present

Responsible for recruiting outstanding engineering and science students from top universities and colleges for the Navy's nuclear surface and submarine officer training programs.

→ In charge of all program budgeting, planning, advertising and direct mail activities for one of the largest recruiting districts in the country.
→ Responsible for interviewing and technical evaluation/screening of applicants.
→ Selected for promotion to Lieutenant Commander.

Main Propulsion Assistant, USS California (CGN 36), San Francisco, CA   9/87-9/88

Qualified as Engineer by the Naval Reactors Division of the U.S. Department of Energy. Managed 60 personnel, two divisions and four work centers as Propulsion Assistant.

→ Served as Main Control Engineering Officer of the watch during general quarters and special operations.
→ Served as Tactical Action Officer, responsible for ship's sensor and weapons while deployed to the North Arabian Sea and Persian Gulf operating areas.
→ Served as ship's Safety Officer, Officer in Charge of the Ship's Damage Control Training Team and Senior Drill Monitor for the ship's Nuclear Training Team.

  - As Nuclear Work Coordinator, scheduled, coordinated and managed steam plant and reactor plant mechanical systems maintenance and repair, specifically:
    Two ion exchange resin and purification filter media discharge and refill evolutions.
  - Five reactor coolant loop drain, evacuation and fill operations to support reactor coolant pump modifications.
  - Numerous reactor plant primary valve repairs and subsequent system hydrostatic tests.
  - Steam generator u-tube eddy-current testing, tube pulls and closeout inspections.
  - Primary and secondary system relief valve adjustment and testing.
  - Main feed pump and main circulation pump overhauls and replacement.

ALFRED E. JOHNSON   **Page Two**

Operations and Deck Division Officer, USS Nimitz CVN-68,
Mayberry, VA   3/85-9/87

→   Ranked #1 of eleven Junior Lieutenants on board.
→   Responsible for managing two divisions (approximately 40 personnel).
→   Qualified Officer of the Deck Underway.
→   Qualified Tactical Action Officer, responsible for employment of the ship's sensors and weapons systems.
→   Top Secret Clearance based on Special Background Investigation.

HONORS: →   Awarded Navy Commendation Medal for superior performance in supervising Nuclear work during USS California's Drydocking.
→   Awarded Navy Achievement Medal for superior performance in supervising emergent propulsion plant repairs while USS California was deployed to the Indian Ocean.
→   Awarded Navy Achievement Medal for superior performance as departmental maintenance and material officer during USS Nimitz overhaul.

EDUCATION: **B.S. Degree, Nuclear Engineering, June 1982**
Northern Illinois University, DeKalb, IL

Navy Nuclear Power Training
Rantail, IL, FL/West Milton, N.Y.
Completed a comprehensive, graduate-level program in the theory, design and operation of naval nuclear reactors.
Qualified to supervise the operation of a naval nuclear reactor plant under normal and emergency conditions.

Mr. Terry Jones

230 S. Draw Lane #112
Schaumburg, IL 60193

708/555-1327

CREATIVE WRITING, DESIGN AND / OR ILLUSTRATION

Experience:

☐ More than two years in professional writing, design and illustration, including full responsibility for creative development, execution and prompt client servicing.

☐ Successful experience in virtually all aspects of creative writing, design, drawing, painting and/or production oversight for:

☞ **T.V., radio, newspaper, magazine and point-of-purchase advertising for major clients...**
☞ **Corporate logos, slogans & tag lines...**
☞ **3-D/graphic designs of all types, especially for brochures, newsletters and trade show themes...**

Employment:

Freelance Copywriter and Artist   2/94-Present
Responsible for creative writing and design of a wide range of promotions for radio, cable & regional T.V., 3-D P.O.P. displays and specialty logos.

☞ Major accounts include Up, Up and Away. Created and executed near life-size illustrations of NBA basketball stars.
☞ Created & executed a logo for Universal West Land Developers.

Prior Experience:

Copywriter/Artist Monet and Associates, Naperville, IL
Performed writing and design work for radio spots, print ads, 3-D work, brochures, newspaper items and full advertising campaigns.

Copywriter/Artist Bertram Marketing Resources, Warrenville, IL
Wrote/designed T.V. and radio ads, slogans and tag lines, designs & Illustrations, brochures, newsletters and magazine ads.
Developed 3-D materials, a sales office design and T.V. and radio ads used by such clients as Sears, Subway and a major Tinley Park land developer.

Designer St. Clair Pakwell, Bellwood, IL
Projects included development of trade show themes, brochures, boxes and bags.

Education & Professional Affiliations:

Ray College of Design, Chicago, IL
Three-Year Associate Degree: Advertising Design
Bachelor's Degree expected 5/95.
GPA: 3.5/4.0.

Samples or photographs of projects available on request

Notes: A very unique design for a creative illustration, design and/or writing position. Terry would take any of the three. We cut this page just within the dotted line to fit perfectly in a personalized, 6"x9" envelope printed with his eye-catching artwork. The lines, pointing hands and 3-D squares on top were created with PageMaker 4.0, a desktop publishing program available for your DOS or Macintosh computer and used by some print and resume shops. The Experience section avoids repetition under each job. We used the jargon of the industry, though sparsely. Terry used "Mr." because he would often be mistaken as female prior to interviews.

ARTHUR D. METAL   *COMBINATION*

220 Albert Lane #F   208/555-5069 Res.
Lansing, MI 17025   208/555-5088 Bus.

OBJECTIVE: ***MANAGEMENT***
A position in the Tool and Die industry where proven leadership skills and hands-on experience would be utilized.

CAREER BACKGROUND:

- Project management skills include production scheduling, SPC/quality control and cost containment.

- Coordinate JIT delivery and cost-effective inventory control.

- Handle staff hiring, training and supervision; effective in job delegation and maintaining positive worker motivation and morale.

- Proven ability to increase sales with new and established clientele through professional communications.

- Assist in developing and updating policies related to worker and management relations.

EMPLOYMENT: <u>Dilbert Fixtures, Inc.,</u> Detroit, MI   8/87-Present
Plant Manager
In charge of all operations related to metal stamping, tool and die work, progressive dies, jigs and fixtures from initial concept to finished product.
Machine line includes punch presses up to 300-ton capacity to produce complex metal parts.

Train and supervise up to 18 employees; schedule work hours and maintain pay rates that are fair to workers and profitable for management.
Consistently schedule, revise and improve production lines; handle temporary/small tooling and troubleshooting.

- Constantly seek to improve working conditions and worker morale through review and upgrading of corporate policies.
- Commended for reducing annual production costs 12 percent.

<u>B.D. Tool Co.,</u> Detroit, MI   9/83-8/87
Contract Tool and Die Maker
Produced tools and dies on a contract basis.
Specialized in class "A" work on a wide variety of products.

<u>Willis Manufacturing Company,</u> Detroit, MI   4/78-9/83
Tool and Die Maker
Established new cost-cutting methods for tool and die fabrication,
including the introduction of more economical materials.

- Implemented a new procedure that lessened die wear due to
  sharpening.
- Significantly increased product quality through production and
  product tracking methods.
- Directly responsible for improving design standards, as well as a 50
  percent decrease in production downtime.

<u>Brandco Tool and Engineering,</u> Detroit, MI   3/71-4/75
                                                          and 6/76-4/78
Diemaker
Assumed responsibilities of owner and manager during vacations and
absences.

- Acted as Group Leader for more than 50 percent of all projects in
  which I was involved.

Previous Employment at shops in the Chicago area, including Remcel
Engineering, Tauber Brothers Tool Company and Kamen Tool and
Engineering.

EDUCATION: <u>Streamwood Community College,</u> Evanston, MI
Completed courses in Liberal Arts
- Successful completion of numerous industry-related courses,
  seminars and workshops.

GARY G. STARBUCKS

COMBINATION

22349 Savoy Court
Schaumburg, IL 60193

708/555-0331

CREDIT / COLLECTIONS MANAGEMENT

EXPERIENCE:

- More than ten years in the management of sales, customer service and production operations, including full profit/loss responsibility.

- Staff hiring, training and supervision in tangible and intangible product sales and service.

- Skilled in strategic planning, marketing and sales staff motivation; experience in sales forecasting, budget management and cost containment.

Credit/Collections:
Manage credit and collection activities. Analyze financial statements and evaluate new accounts; organize database systems for specific business needs.

Customer Service:
Manage telephone and mail order customer service operations; train staff in customer problem resolution, professional communications and full client servicing.

Management:
Plan and implement sales, service and cost reduction procedures; work directly with senior-level personnel in budget administration, distribution and materials management.

Sales:
Effectively hire, train and supervise sales and marketing teams in technical product lines, sales presentations and market penetration.

EMPLOYMENT: Walter Sales Company, Berwyn, IL   9/83-Present
Credit/Collections Manager
Supervise all credit, collections and customer service operations, involving the supervision of more than 28 employees for this major manufacturer and wholesaler of automotive after- market products.
Manage all aspects of order processing/expediting, billing and account updating on a WANG system.
Coordinate technical problem solving and customer correspondence via ACD telephone, fax and mail.

* Responsible for all operations and facilities in absence of company owners.
* Developed and implemented the key account sales and service program.

Singer Safety Company, Chicago, IL   10/80-9/83
Customer Service and Credit/Collections Manager
Effectively managed 22 employees in order processing, client relations and account servicing.
Directed credit research on new accounts and established new accounts within credit limitations.
Supervised follow-up on accounts receivable collection activities.

Wilson Sporting Goods Company, Elk Grove Village, IL   8/78-9/80
Assistant Regional Merchandise Manager
In charge of an entire distribution center and all office staff for the midwestern region.
Managed order processing on a corporate-wide computer system, including data entry, account management and customer service.
Updated and maintained accurate inventories on a regular basis.

Performance Dynamics International, Chicago, IL   1/75-8/78
Customer Service and Inside Sales Manager
Trained and motivated sales staff in new account acquisition and management.
Supervised customer relations and special assignments for the CEO.

Sears Roebuck and Company, Chicago, IL   3/66-12/74
Customer Service and Credit Manager
Managed a complete telephone and mail order operation.
Analyzed and improved customer service procedures and sales promotions.
* Developed cost reduction techniques for product deliveries and installations.

EDUCATION: Loyola University, Chicago, IL
Successful completion of courses in Business Administration.

Dale Carnegie Institute
Completed training in Public Speaking, Dynamics of Human Relations, Sales Administration, Credit and Collection Management.
* Conducted courses as Graduate Student Instructor.

Dun and Bradstreet
Completed courses in credit and collection management, including financial statement analysis and customer service management.

CHRISTINA B. CRACKERS

DETAILED CHRONOLOGICAL

226 Alsip Lane
Chicago, IL 60689
312/555-8873

CAREER BACKGROUND

MANAGER: PUBLIC RELATIONS

Bluebird Singer Inc, Chicago, IL   12/86-Present

Developed and implemented a national product publicity program for retail line of audio programs. Determined communications tactics, worked with best-selling authors and supervised creation of print and radio media lists to gain article placements in the nation's top 16 markets.

Placed media in *USA Today, Ladies Home Journal, The Chicago Tribune* and *The Oakland Tribune.*

*   Coordinated a trade-for-mention program with the top-ranked radio station in Chicago; garnered $8,000 worth of promotional air time.
*   Assisted with a press party and publicity for a video with Chicago Cub Andre Dawson.
*   Responsible for trade media relations. Efforts resulted in 13 placements in a leading industry publication, including 12 product reviews in 1988.

Special Events and Advertising: Coordinated key customer breakfasts with authors at trade shows. Plan and implement trade and direct response print advertisements.

Marketing: Oversee all aspects of production for product packaging and sales promotional materials, involving detailed copy writing and editing under strict deadlines.

DIRECTOR OF PUBLIC RELATIONS

Evanston Commons Association, Evanston, IL   7/84-4/86

This is a nonprofit social service agency with 10 facilities throughout Chicago.
Planned and managed all events for ECA's 90th Anniversary Celebration, including writing the president's speech and organizing a dinner and dance.
Acted as association liaison to two board of directors' committees.

Marketing: Supervised the fall direct mail solicitation campaign and increased contributions by 21 percent over the previous year.

Special Events: Worked directly with board members in the coordination of a Celebrity Birthday Party. Successfully organized an anniversary year festival for service recipients and the "What I Like Best About My Neighborhood" children's art contest.
Personally secured WLS-TV as cosponsor.

*   Generated publicity resulting in 3.8 million media impressions.
*   Gained underwriting from Southland Corporation for two consecutive years for the Christmas Cheer Dinner Giveaway.
*   Arranged the distribution of 432 dinners to the needy.

Media Relations: Responsible for more than 30 print placements in major publications including *The Washington Post.*

Publications / Special Projects: Performed writing, editing and production supervision for a special anniversary annual report and various newsletters.
* Writer of the winning entry in the United Way/Rothschild Heart of Gold Award Program for outstanding community volunteers.

ASSISTANT REGIONAL MARKETING MANAGER
Reader's Digest Services, Inc., Chicago, IL   10/82-6/84
Marketing: Assisted in writing and preparing a six-month sales/marketing plan and comprehensive sales reports.
Handled full coordination of assignments between corporate office, regional manager and six field sales representatives.

* Initiated a sales promotion with the district manager and boosted sales 10 percent.

Media Relations: Worked with district managers and facilitated local media relations and special issue presentations.

ASSOCIATIONS

Hugh O'Brian Youth Foundation: Public Relations Director for the Illinois State Leadership Seminar for outstanding high school sophomores, 1986.
Program Committee Member: International Assoc. of Business Communicators, 1987.

EDUCATION

Northern Illinois University, DeKalb, IL
Bachelor of Arts Degree   1982
Major: Journalism/Public Relations; Minor: Political Science

* Freelance experience included:
  Writer: *The Near East Gazette.* Gained front-page position with news reporting on controversies surrounding local real estate developments.
  Consultant: The Children's Home & Aid Society of Illinois. Provided creative services for the 1986 annual report.

INTERNSHIPS and HONORS

Winner of the Ralph Edwards Outstanding Senior in Public Relations Award from the
Public Relations Society of America (PRSA), 1982.
National Citation for Outstanding Chapter Service, The Public Relations Student Society of America (PRSSA), 1983.
President, PRSSA, Northern Illinois University Chapter.
Intern: The Burson-Marsteller, Inc., Professional Partners Program.

SYLVIA M. MYERSKI   *CHRONOLOGICAL*

826 Elgin Lane
Geneva, TX 69483   508/555-3821

OBJECTIVE: A position in ***Product Management,*** where proven technical skills would be utilized.

EXPERIENCE: <u>DataLink Systems, Inc.</u>, Scoreville, TX   10/87-Present
                    Product Manager
                    In charge of directing new product planning and development activities for this Fortune 500 firm, including the development and implementation of comprehensive marketing strategies and plans.
                    Administer budgets for media and product introduction materials.
                    Plan and conduct competitive product and market share analyses.
                    Research, produce and update catalogs and price lists.
                    - Developed a detailed product cost and selling price spreadsheet.
                    - Provide full support in the training of sales personnel.

                    <u>UNIX Corporation</u>, Austin, TX   9/85-10/87
                    Product Line Manager - Payment Systems Division
                    Completely responsible for the preparation of marketing plans for new credit authorization terminals.
                    Designed innovative advertising/promotional literature, including slides and trade show exhibits.
                    - Wrote comprehensive system programming, installation and operation manuals.
                    - Developed and successfully implemented customer training programs.
                    - Directly involved in the research and development of new products, including the planning, coordination and testing of future software releases.

                    <u>Motorola Corporation</u>, Austin, TX   7/83-9/85
                    Peripheral Product Coordinator
                    Coordinated production of the NGC MultiSync monitor, including research of market potential and preparation of a comprehensive marketing plan.
                    Evaluated preproduction printers and monitors for performance and specification compliance.
                    - Researched and wrote detailed, annotated operational manuals.
                    - Established a product tracking system for the entire sales force.

EDUCATION: <u>University of Texas</u>, Austin, TX
                    B.S. Degree: Marketing   Graduated 5/83
                    - President of business administration student council
                    - Elected as Honors Convocation Speaker and Emcee for the Business College.

ASSOCIATIONS: Member: Phi Chi Theta Professional Fraternity and the American Marketing Association.

BETTY WHITE
570 Bourbon Street,
Tacoma, WA 98176
206/555-0257

COMBINATION

LEGAL SECRETARY
A position where professional skills and a knowledge of legal terms would be utilized.

PROFILE:

▸ Secretary and Receptionist experience includes research, correspondence writing, client relations and payroll processing.

▸ Skilled in MS Word, WordPerfect and WordStar as well as Lotus 1-2-3; familiar with WestLaw and Lexus; operate various switchboard systems and compile/produce detailed reports via dictaphone.

▸ Interface with legal staff and handle general accounting, bookkeeping and special projects in a professional manner.

CAREER BACKGROUND:

Holtz and Reinhart, Tacoma, WA   7/90-Present
Legal Secretary
Currently providing assistance in case studies and the research, preparation and updating of a wide variety of legal documents.
Operate a 12-line switchboard; write/expedite messages and handle greeting and reception of clients.
Write/type correspondence related to legal matters using WordPerfect.

Seattle, WA   4/83-7/90
Homemaker

Omaha Bank, Omaha, NE   11/79-4/83
Payroll Clerk   4/80-4/83
Maintained accuracy of over 400 time cards and processed computer input forms and reports.
Utilized MSA and ADP computer systems, as well as Addressograph equipment.

· Scheduled data processing projects and checked/distributed pay stubs; processed salary changes and updated life insurance cards.
· Developed microfilm and typed/produced monthly life insurance reports; processed employee's Savings Bonds.

Receptionist/Secretary   11/79-4/80
Primarily responsible for letter and memo typing from Dictaphone and rough drafts.
Worked directly with senior-level personnel on special projects.

EDUCATION: Alberts College, Seattle, WA
Completed the Legal Secretary Program   Diploma, 1985

SYLVESTER BRIDGES   *COMBINATION*
9291 Shaver Drive
Minneapolis, MN 30090
608/555-6858

SALES / SALES MANAGEMENT

EXPERIENCE

- More than 15 years in sales and sales management, including proven success with leading manufacturing firms in major metropolitan markets.

- Handle comprehensive research and competitive analysis for the implementation of strategic marketing plans.

- Assist in staff training and supervision with excellent communication skills; develop a strong "team" atmosphere among sales reps and support personnel.

- Determine and meet client's specific business needs; plan and conduct sales presentations with key clientele in a professional, yet personalized manner.

- Demonstrated success in the development of long-term business partnerships.

EMPLOYMENT

Flasho Manufacturing, Minneapolis, MN   1987-Present
Midwest District Sales Manager   1988-Present
Responsible for sales to mass merchants for this home textile marketer, which has a national client base generating $100 million annually.
Work directly with merchants at major chains, department stores, supermarkets and drug stores.
Manage budgets, determine sales quotas and penetration strategies and monitor co-op advertising efforts on a regular basis. Effectively train and supervise a broker sales force and various company representatives.

* Personally handle major accounts including J.C. Penney, Walgreens, Kohls, Osco Drug, Pamida, Shopko, Meijers and Cotter & Company,
* Increased sales from $800,000 to $3.5 million, 1987-Present.
* Established productive relationships with major accounts resulting in a dramatic rebound in the Midwest territory.
* Hired and trained a new sales representative for Program Selling in Indianapolis, resulting in a dramatic sales increase for a previously dormant territory.
* Promoted to this position from **Senior Midwest Account Executive,** 1987-1988.

The Bale Company, A division of Sears Roebuck, Hackensack, NJ   1984-1987
Chicago Regional Sales Manager   1985-1987
Management duties included the development of buying plans and sales forecasts for this manufacturer of intimate apparel.

* Trained and supervised four sales associates & field merchandisers working with major accounts such as K-Mart, Carson Pirie Scott and other retailers.

Key Account Sales Representative - Chicago/Milwaukee 1984-1985
Responsible for key account sales to major department stores.
Maintained direct communication with buying staff and senior store management regarding volume and profitability.
Trained and supervised three sales associates.

Harold Rice & Associates, Niles, NY 1983-1984
Account Executive
Called directly on national advertisers to plan and implement marketing and communication programs.
Worked primarily with point-of-purchase displays and package designs, as well as sales promotions and related materials.

Playtex, Inc., New York, NY 1981-1983
Key Account Sales Representative - Chicago/Milwaukee
Responsible for the sale of branded product lines to major department stores, as well as specialty and military accounts. Presented national promotions for new products and programs.
Developed/implemented effective buying plans and generated monthly reorders.
Supervised one merchandiser and maintained excellent communications with key accounts.

* Instrumental in launching marketing campaigns that increased sales and service demands.
* Acted as liaison between company and accounts to provide timely information, expedite service and resolve conflicts.
* Increased sales volume 12 percent, 1981-1983.

Ralph Meyers Intimate Apparel Company, Inc., New York, NY 1973-1981
Field Sales Representative
Conducted high-volume sales to major department stores, as well as military and specialty accounts.
Involved in all phases of direct sales, including program development, inventory control and customer relations.

* Recognized for excellent sales performance.
* Increased sales volume in last assigned territory by $315,000.

EDUCATION

Northeastern University, Chicago, IL
Bachelor of Arts Degree: Marketing 1973

Xerox Corporation
Completed the Selling Skills II course. 1984

PERSONAL

Willing to travel extensively or relocate.

JOHN S. RAZZ   *CHRONOLOGICAL*

2751 Autumn Road East   512/555-6765 Res.
Salem, OR 94305   512/555-8590 Bus.

EXPERIENCE:

Executive Director   1989-Present
Christians for Youth Initiatives, Eugene, OR
In charge of all activities for this nonprofit organization providing resources and training nationwide for children 11-14 years of age.

Area Manager   1988
Alpha Products, Inc., Salem, OR
Managed sales and marketing for this manufacturer of security systems and real estate lock boxes.

Associate Director of University Relations   1983-1987
William University, Salem, OR
Coordinated fundraising programs for Mark O. Hatfield Library, centerpiece of a $22.5 million capital campaign.
Promoted to this position from **Director of Alumni Relations**.

Assistant to the Vice President   1981-1982
The University of South Carolina, Columbia, SC
Wrote proposals and conducted research for cooperative programs between the University, the State of South Carolina, private industry, the federal government and foreign countries.

Legislative Assistant   1976-1981
U.S. Senator Mark D. Rogers, Washington, DC
Acted as director and advisor to the Senator on issues including education, defense, transportation and world hunger.
Prepared speeches, floor statements and background papers, as well as appearances on behalf of Senator Mark Rogers.
Acted as office liaison to individuals and groups in Oregon seeking action or assistance from U.S. government departments.

*   Served as campaign Field Director for the Committee to Re-Elect Mark O. Hatfield in the Senator's successful senate race of 1978.
*   Gained hands-on experience in public speaking and the writing, preparation and distribution of correspondence, promotional materials and mass mailings.
*   Planned itineraries in compliance with state and local regulations.

Internship   1976
The Dixie Endowment of Indianapolis, IN
Conducted research and program evaluation in the Divisions of Education and Religion.
Directly involved in projects related to values and the liberal arts, as well as in various religion-oriented activities and programs.

Student Member   1975
The Oregon Educational Council, Salem, OR
Appointed by the Governor of Oregon and confirmed by the State Senate to serve as the first student member of the Oregon Educational Coordinating Council with full voting privileges.
This council is charged with the coordination, planning and evaluation of Oregon's educational system.

College Admissions Representative   Summers, 1974-1975
Warner Pacific College, Salem, OR
Conducted speeches and contacted/counseled prospective students.
Traveled to youth camps, conventions and churches throughout the United States and Canada.

EDUCATION:

M.Ed. Degree   1982
Graduate degree in Higher Education Administration
Student Personnel Services
University of Carolina, Columbia, SC

B.A. Degree   1975
Major: Religious Studies
* Elected student body President, senior year
Warner Pacific College, Salem, OR

Volunteer Work:

The Institute for Christian Leadership and Renewal, Salem, OR
This institute aids in the development of new clusters of Christian colleges.
1980-1982
Americans for International Aid and Adoption, Salem, OR
Escorting orphaned children from India and Korea to their new adopted homes in the U.S.
1982 - Present

Professional Affiliations:

Member: Council for the Advancement & Support of Education (CASE).
Member: Greater Salem Young Life Committee
Member: 1983 Campaign Cabinet, United Way of the Mid-Wilmette Valley
Member: Yokefellows International
Former Member: City Club of Portland
Former Associate Director: Portland Rose Festival Association

THOMAS F. MAJORS   *COMBINATION/Smaller Summary*

2551 Purple Lane
Aurora, CO 20004   908/555-5134

EXPERIENCE:
- Excellent driver with an accident-free record; skilled in forklift driving.
- Bachelor of Science in Education, with a concentration in Math and Science.
- Completion of Auto Mechanics and Technical courses.

EMPLOYMENT: United Parcel Service,   10/86-1/89 and 6/89-1/93
Bedford, CO
Package Handler (part-time)
Various duties included forklift driving and unloading trailers on a busy dock.
Switched trailers for approximately three months.
Worked in a fast-paced environment.

Robert's Limousine Service   6/89-1/90
Crown Point, CO
Bus Driver (part-time)
Safely transported college students to and from work and home.

Elm Lawn Cemetery   5/88-8/88 and 6/89-8/89
Schererville, CO
Groundskeeper (part-time)
Updated and maintained the appearance of cemetery property.

Continental Armature   5/86-6/86
Blue Island, CO
Armature Rebuilder
Rebuilt starter motor armatures, involving operation of a cutting lathe, sanding, buffing and testing for quality control.

VOLUNTEER
SERVICES: Spanish Sunday School Teacher's Assistant.
Volunteer Bus Driver for a college transportation department.

EDUCATION: Calvin Dilbert College
Crown Point, IN
Bachelor of Science Degree in Secondary Education   Graduated May, 1990

Hoyne Technical Institute
Completed 20 weeks of training in auto mechanics.

INTERESTS: Enjoy scuba diving, hiking, fishing and intramural football.

GRACE N. MICHAELS   *COMBINATION*

32275 Plum Creek Lane
Boulder, CO 40090   908/555-7542

___

OBJECTIVE: A position where professional RN skills would be utilized.

EXPERIENCE: ■   More than seven years in nursing, including six years in a psychiatric unit.

                    ■   Create and implement individual and group therapy programs; plan and supervise counseling sessions for the milieu.

                    ■   Experience in primary nursing for trauma, med/surg, pediatric, child/adolescent and psychiatric units.

                    ■   Working toward Master's Degree and Certification in Diabetic Teaching.

EMPLOYMENT: <u>Northwest Community Hospital,</u> Denver, CO   10/90-Present
                    Staff RN
                    Responsible for primary nursing in a 39-bed med/surg pediatric unit.
                    *   Instruct new diabetics on symptom assessment and alleviation.
                    *   Active member of the Shared Governance Council for this unit.

                    <u>Denver General Hospital,</u> Denver, CO   10/89-7/90
                    Staff LPN
                    Involved in successful team nursing, primarily in a trauma unit.
                    Floated as needed to the adolescent psychiatric unit.

                    <u>West Pines Psychiatric Hospital,</u> Wheat Ridge, CO   1/89-1/90
                    Mental Health Counselor
                    In charge of the milieu on a daily basis.
                    Handled patient assessments and performed group and individual counseling.
                    *   Assisted in the children's unit and floated to the adolescent unit as needed.

                    <u>Children's Hospital,</u> Denver, CO   12/88-1/90
                    Mental Health Counselor

                    <u>Fort Logan Mental Health Center,</u> Denver, CO   6/87-10/88
                    Mental Health Counselor
                    As counselor and milieu specialist, conducted one-on-one sessions with individual patients and maintained a safe, therapeutic environment.
                    Performed low- and high-level interventions including RMA, TP, limit setting, seclusion and 4-6 pointing a patient.
                    Organized and managed role-playing groups, issue & rap sessions and young women's groups.
                    *   Designed/structured milieu activities; acted as mediator between patient and case coordinator and charted daily/weekly patient progress.
                    *   Supervised off-unit recreational therapy groups and a special snack program.
                    *   Earned Patient Appreciation Award.

GRACE N. MICHAELS Page Two

<u>City and County of Denver,</u> Denver, CO 9/84-8/87
Case Service Aide III
Performed one-on-one sessions with children having conduct disorders and restrained them when necessary.
Admitted children from birth to 12 years of age; documented their history and examined them for bruises and marks.
* Provided support for physically and sexually abused children through small groups and education.
* Designed and implemented structured play activities and craft projects.
* Conducted feelings/values clarification groups.
* Provided a nurturing, stimulating atmosphere for failure-to-thrive children.

<u>The Baptist Home Association,</u> Wheat Ridge, CO 9/84-11/84
Nurse's Aide
Attended to ADLs of elderly patients and performed colostomy care.
Provided positive reinforcement and a caring atmosphere.

**VOLUNTEER
EXPERIENCE:** <u>Volunteers of America,</u> Denver, CO 1986
Supervised activities at the Bannock Shelter for adolescent boys.

<u>Channel 9 Health Fair,</u> Denver, CO 4/87
Participant

EDUCATION: <u>Loretto Heights College,</u> Denver, CO
B.S. Degree - Nursing 5/87
* Worked with the Denver Social Services Sex Abuse Team.
* Taught childhood safety and developmental stages to a new mother in her own home.
* Attended numerous seminars offered by Denver Social Services and the Fort Logan Mental Health Center:

- Milieu Management   - Psychotropic Drugs
- Borderline Personality - Therapeutic Relationships
- Separation Anxiety   - Legal Restraints
- O.T. Therapy   - Failure to Thrive Children
- The Deaf Child and How to Communicate
- Sexual Abuse: Signs and Symptoms
- Plain Talk About Dealing with the Angry Child
- Play Therapy for the Sexually Abused Child

**AWARDS &
ACHIEVEMENTS:**

* Alpha Chi National Honor Scholarship Society
* High Honors: Dean's List
* Loretto Heights College Scholarship
* Maintained 3.25/4.0 GPA while working at least 30 hours a week and raising four children.

STEPHEN PETERS   *COMBINATION*

22546 Elk Horn Lane
Peoria, IL 60090   708/555-3215

OBJECTIVE:	A position in Counseling where professional communication skills would be utilized.

PROFILE:

- Proven ability to communicate with juveniles from age 12, adult prison inmates, gang members and DCFS wards.

- Perform individual counseling, problem assessment and documentation; develop and schedule group activities.

- Provide active, ongoing support and guidance as an effective listener.

EMPLOYMENT:

DuPage Temporary Juvenile Detention Center, Chicago, IL   1990-Present
Children's Attendant
Responsible for counseling and maintaining law and order for 16 boys age 12-16.

Last Chance Mortgage Corporation, Wheeling, IL   1987-1990
Customer Service Representative
Communicated directly with the clientele regarding account balances, payment due dates and customer complaints.
Operated a computer system for account tracking and updating.

VOLUNTEER WORK:

Little City Group, Chicago, IL   1990-Present
Counselor
Directly involved in counseling prison inmates on personal problems and documenting their living conditions at numerous state correctional centers.

MILITARY:

U.S. Army, **Sergeant - 2nd Armor Division**   1983-1987
Trained and supervised noncommissioned officers.
Performed scheduling and accounting for soldiers; authorized passes and dealt with A.W.O.L. soldiers.
*   Counseled soldiers facing disciplinary actions and referred them to special organizations in cases of marriage or divorce.

EDUCATION:

Brown College, Palatine, IL   1988-Present
Completion of courses in Criminal Justice, Sociology, Mathematics, Psychology and Racquetball.

Central Texas College, Killeen, TX   1986-1987
Courses included Public Speaking, College Algebra, Psychology, Public Speaking and English.

High School Graduate   1986

HAROLD P. PATRICK   *FUNCTIONAL*

2337 Brasher Court
Northbrook, IL 60062   708/555-0182

ENGINEERING / FACILITY MANAGEMENT

PROFESSIONAL HIGHLIGHTS:

EFFICIENCY:
- Design and install conveyor systems that ease work flow and increase production.
- Installed computer systems proven to cut production time of weekly invoices in half. Redesigned an invoice to accommodate office, production and delivery procedures more efficiently.
- Invented a pry-bar that cut a company's manual demolition time by one-third.
- Extensive experience with high pressure boilers, three-phase electricity, pipe fitting, pneumatic and electric controls, pump/motor repair and welding.
- Work with job shops to fabricate or repair obsolete and expensive parts to keep 30-year-old equipment operating.
- Skilled in the use of WordStar and Quattro for word processing and the compilation of financial data.

MANAGEMENT:
- Supervise all phases of operations including production, inventory control and maintenance.
- Work directly with inspectors, union officials, OSHA personnel, auditors and attorneys. Administer EEOC regulations and right-to-know legislation.
- Experience supervising union and non-English speaking employees.
- Act as insurance risk manager: obtain quotes, maintain policies, verify audits and file workmen's compensation reports.
- Work with general contractors, architects and engineers; develop plans for building construction and remodeling projects valued up to $500,000.
- Serve as on-site coordinator for all trades while supervising plant operations.
- Skilled in the selection, design, installation and operation of waste water pretreatment systems. Represent companies at Sanitary District hearings. Apply for local, state and federal regulatory permits and file subsequent reports.

Harold P. Patrick   **Page Two**

EMPLOYMENT HISTORY:

1989 - 1990   **Project Manager**, Bison Cleaners
                   Large retail facility with annual sales of $1.5 million.

1963 - 1989   **Plant Manager**, The Uniform Rental Service
                   Industrial laundry with annual sales of $3 million.

1970 - 1972   **SP-5,** U.S. Army (Vietnam)
                   Honorably Discharged.

LICENSES

City of Chicago **Stationary Engineer's License**

EDUCATION

Bachelor of Science, Southern Illinois University, Carbondale, IL, 1968

CONTINUING EDUCATION

Completed Studies in:

Robotics
Stationary Engineering
Computers
Welding
Machine Shop Math

MARK STRUCTURE   *COMBINATION*

1123 Edwards Lane
Clearwater, FL 30025
308/555-8769

PROPERTY MANAGEMENT

PROFESSIONAL EXPERIENCE

▸ More than four years in property management, including full responsibility for contractor scheduling, budget management, lease negotiation and extensive commercial/residential customer relations.

▸ Handle market research and the coordination of cost-effective advertising, marketing and promotional programs.

▸ Skilled in staff hiring, training and supervision; compile and present detailed status reports and analyze related expenditures.

▸ Utilize MS Word and ProWrite to produce resident and investor correspondence; organize billing and invoicing procedures to meet specific business needs.

CAREER BACKGROUND

Superior Management Corporation, Glenview, FL   4/88-3/95

Property Manager   9/88-3/95

Coordinate all promotional, leasing and maintenance activities for a 17-story, combined residential/commercial use building on Chicago's Gold Coast.
Hired and managed a staff of seven including maintenance personnel and doormen; conducted regular performance reviews of all employees.
Managed all budgets and screened & hired subcontractors and tradesmen; compiled and distributed lease expiration and weekly traffic/activity reports to all investors.

- Maintained a 99 percent occupancy rate through effective advertising and sales presentations.
- Assisted in legal proceedings as needed for evictions and delinquent accounts.
- Promoted to this position from **Receptionist:** 4/88-9/88.

Inland Development, Deerfield, FL   3/85-4/88

Project Coordinator

Interfaced with buyers and construction contractors building customized, single-family homes.
Assisted in selecting options, preparing contracts and assuring the quality of completed work.

NANCY A. GRAHAM

COMBINATION

70 Kenneth Circle
Hope, AK 30129

528/555-2258

OBJECTIVE:
Continued career growth in the Food and Lodging industry.
Particular areas of interest include Accounting, Management, Marketing and Regional or District Office Operations.

PROFILE:
- Proven ability to train and supervise up to 50 employees; experience as General Manager of two economy hotels.
- Trained in profit/loss balancing and long- & short-term budget planning.

EXPERIENCE:

HOLIDAY INNS OF AMERICA   10/89-Present
Hope, AK
General Manager
Effectively supervise 20 employees, including hiring, training and scheduling.
Oversee front desk, maintenance and housekeeping personnel.
Maintain accurate inventories and order all necessary supplies.
Handle billing for corporate accounts and handle sales, including group bookings.

BLUE TIDE INNS   3/87-8/89
Shreveport, LA   9/88-8/89
General Manager
Responsible for hiring, training and supervising up to 18 employees.
In charge of front desk operations, housekeeping staff and the assistant manager.
Improved budget process and sales through effective balancing of profits and losses.
Maintained inventory and ordered supplies.

Dallas/Carrolton, TX   4/88-9/88
Assistant Manager
Accepted full responsibility for inventory, payroll and P&L of the operation.
Trained and supervised ten employees in all customer service and sales activities.

Downers Grove, IL   5/87-4/88
Assistant Manager
Similar duties to those described above with a staff of 23.

Trainee

PONDEROSA STEAK HOUSE   10/86-5/87
Downers Grove, IL
Manager
Promoted to a new "turn-around" management team at this store, plagued by poor performance.
Responsibilities included the supervision and scheduling of 35-55 employees in stocking, inventory control, reordering and direct customer service.

* Staff recruiting and training was a major part of this position and the key to improved profits.
* Personally created recruiting programs and conducted presentations at high schools, trade shows and health departments.
* Planned and implemented training programs and evaluated worker progress.
* As a result of these actions, employee morale improved and turnover decreased 20%.
* Quality control was upgraded and traffic volume increased 15%.

PONDEROSA STEAK HOUSE   10/84-10/85
Elgin, IL
Assistant Manager
Similar duties as above while training.

SAGA CORPORATION   Summers and Breaks,
W.I.U., Northfield, IL   1982-1984
Cook's Helper/Key Student
Prepared and served salads and beverages in this part-time position.

EDUCATION: WESTERN ILLINOIS UNIVERSITY, Macomb, IL
Bachelor of Science Degree in Food and Nutrition   Graduated 5/84
Specialization: Food and Lodging   Minor: Business

Business subjects included marketing, management, human resources and accounting.
Utilized a Macintosh computer and WordPerfect 5.1.
Activities: Food Committee Representative, 1982.
Western Illinois Ski Club, 1980-1983 (Vice President 1982-1983).
Earned Sanitation Certificate, State of Illinois, 1984.

**ADDITIONAL
TRAINING:** Earned Certificates from Blue Tide Inns for completion of:
Management Training Program, 1987
Motivating and Team Building, 1989
Coaching & Developing the Assistant Manager, 1989
Interaction Management Seminar, 1988
Hospitality Seminar, 1988

PERSONAL: Willing to travel or relocate. Enjoy reading, bowling, darts and water/snow skiing.

PAUL A. MOCKI   *ENTRY-LEVEL COMBINATION*

1123 Northern Pines Drive
Saugatuck, MI 90070   348/555-9100

OBJECTIVE: A position with an environmentally conscious organization, where communication and managerial skills would be utilized.

**KEY SKILLS
and ABILITIES:**
- Trained in report preparation, laboratory research, bookkeeping and general business administration.

- Skilled in the use of Macintosh and DOS systems; utilize WordPerfect and Lotus 1-2-3; handle customer service, speeches and presentations in a professional manner.

EDUCATION: Bison College of Waupaca, Waupaca, WI
                    Bachelor of Arts Degree: Environmental Biology   August, 1991
* Lab work included comprehensive studies of water chemistry.
* Created a detailed, hypothetical land use plan.
* WAISE Scholarship Recipient, 1990
* Completed an Undergraduate Thesis on Solid Waste Management. Examined waste management decisions affecting the environment. Conducted extensive research and interviewed state, city and county representatives.
Analyzed the politics of environmental decision making and presented findings.

* Courses included hands-on experience in:
  - Physics   - Telemetry   - Ornithology
  - Botany   - Zoology   - Ecology

EMPLOYMENT: The Nightclub Hotel, Winona, MN   June, 1990-Present
                    Night Auditor
In charge of all hotel activities during night shift, including bookkeeping and direct customer service for this hotel with 136 rooms and a restaurant.
Work directly with vendors; process accounts payable and cash receipts.
Supervise guest groups; handle check-ins/outs and assist the manager in all operations.

                    Blue Trail Nature Center, Winona, MN   Summer, 1989
                    Naturalist
Acted as an information resource to the public and presented interpretative talks regarding nature and the Forest Preserve District.
Cared for Nature Center animals, assisted in construction projects and maintained nature center grounds and trails.

**Previous
Employment:**   White Castle, Mt. Prospect, MN   Summer, 1988
                    Crewperson Provided efficient, quality service for all customers.
* Recognized as Crewperson of the Month for May, 1991.

                    Bison College of Waupaca, Waupaca, MN   Summer, 1987
                    Maintenance Worker

GIUSEPPE L. MIRAND   *COMBINATION*

2223 August Square Road
Barrington, IL 60193   708/555-3174

PROFILE:
- More than 14 years in accounting, including responsibility for department procedures, budgets and computer operations.

- Train and supervise staff in accounting activities and the use of Lotus 3.1 and Supercalc 5; familiar with full system conversions.

- Plan and conduct audits and variance analyses; process payrolls and personal & corporate taxes; update and maintain accurate inventories.

EMPLOYMENT:

Scarpendous Displays, Inc., An exhibit setup & service firm
Accounting Manager   Chicago, IL 12/93-Present
Responsible for the accurate, timely processing of accounts payable/receivable, payroll, insurance & union reports and sales/payroll tax returns.
Perform job costing, account analysis and general ledger maintenance using Lotus 1-2-3 and Excel.
* Instrumental in converting from an IBM System 34 to a Novell Network.
* Prepare monthly and annual financial statements.

Lancer Systems, Manufacturing
Accounting Manager   Elk Grove, IL 1/88-9/93
Trained and supervised five employees in accounting activities.
Analyzed and interpreted forecasts, capital expenditures and financial data.
Directly involved in budget preparation and coordination.
* Evaluated operational systems and procedures, as well as financial reporting methods on a regular basis.
* Analyzed cost variances and monitored intercompany transactions.
* Supervised a conversion using AS400 and Lotus 1-2-3.

Coopers & Lybrand, Public Accounting
Senior Accountant   Chicago, IL 6/82-12/87
Performed detailed financial audits of numerous businesses and recommended improvements in client's system procedures, documentation and internal controls.
Conducted reviews and compilations.
Prepared corporate and individual income tax returns, payroll and sales taxes.

U.S. Riley Corporation, Manufacturing
Cost Accountant   Skokie, IL 9/81-5/82
Assisted in budget forecasting and developing standard cost data and variance analyses.
Reviewed capital expenditures and coordinated/reconciled physical inventories.

EDUCATION:

Ridgetown College, Venezuela
B.S. Degree: Accounting   1981

WILLIAM DiNERO   *COMBINATION*

324 Bush Street
Bartlett, RI 30103   321/555-1835

SOFTWARE DESIGN / DEVELOPMENT

A position utilizing extensive technical experience
applicable to new products challenges.

PROFILE:

- More than eleven years in software and hardware development, including full responsibility for detailed system documentation and troubleshooting.

- Skilled in 6502 and 68000 Assembler, Turbo Assembler, Turbo C, Fortran, BASIC, Schema II+, Tango PCB and high-speed digital hardware.

EMPLOYMENT:

Pacific Light & Magic, Inc., Nashville, CA   1985-Present
Directed the setup and operation of this firm specializing in the design of state-of-the-art, computerized lighting controllers.
Designed and developed a variety of products including hardware platforms and embedded, real-time software for controller systems.
Wrote/created system documentation and a 200-page user's manual, complete with illustrations.
Negotiated contracts and worked successfully with financial and manufacturing representatives for system production and sales through an outside firm.

* Created a product simulator enabling a Turbo XT to read an industry standard serial data stream and reflect this information in a real-time graphics display. Utilized Turbo C and Turbo Assembler to develop a custom program that included high-speed drivers for serial communications and EGA graphics. This enabled the simulator to meet the requirements of a 250 KB data input rate and a 20 HZ screen refresh rate.

General PowerSoft Company, St. Louis, MO   1984-1985
Performed detailed software and hardware design for defense applications.
Handled all aspects of design and development embedded real-time 77000 assembly code used on a 68000-based hardware card, which acted as an administrator for an image processing subsystem consisting of 10 dedicated hardware boards.

* The 68000 board also communicated with a ROLM military computer, which acted as the administrator for the entire system, an advanced target cuing system to be used on U.S. M-1A1 tanks.
* Successfully designed and developed a video memory card that interfaced an RS 170 video output with a series of dedicated hardware cards used to incorporate various image processing algorithms.

EDUCATION:

University of Illinois, Urbana-Champaign, IL   1984
B.S. Degree, Electrical Engineering   * Dean's List
Admitted to Tau Beta Pi Engineering Honor Society

BETSY WANDERS   *COMBINATION*

235182 Reddy Lane
Sommerville, NJ 10565   328/555-7434

OBJECTIVE: A position utilizing RN, Technical and Analytical skills and which offers the potential for advancement to Head Nurse. *(or: the potential for advancement)*

EXPERIENCE:
- More than five years in oncology, surgical and cardiac units, including full responsibility for patient care and documentation.

- Plan and conduct patient and staff in-services in a professional manner; recognized for providing efficient, personalized patient care.

- Compile and present care plans and written reports with strong analytical skills; organize data on computerized systems; utilize WordPerfect and Lotus to produce charts and graphs.

EMPLOYMENT: Supra Clinic Health Care, Newark, NJ   Pt. Time, 3/91-Present
Home Health Nurse
Perform comprehensive, in-home care for oncology patients.
Duties include the setup of infusion pumps, drawing blood, monitoring morphine intake and regular tracking of patient progress.

Nurse Outsourcers, Aurora, NJ   Pt. Time, 1/90-Present
Nurse
Provide professional care at a variety of hospitals while attending college.
Assist in surgical, orthopedic, cardiac and neurology departments.

Aurora Hospital, Aurora, NJ   5/87-1/90
Staff Nurse - Oncology and Hematology Departments
Responsible for 5 to 10 patients daily, including regular administration of chemotherapy and related I.V.s.
Dispensed whole blood, platelets and cryoprecipitate; maintained access to central venous catheters.
* Provided special care for radiation implant patients.
* Planned and presented in-services for patients and staff; topics included dealing with side effects of radiation therapy, catheter maintenance and the setup of home infusion pumps.
* Nominated by four different patients for the H.E.R.O Award.

EDUCATION: Malta College, Malta, NJ   1987
Associate Degree - Nursing
* Earned Scholarships from the Waterman Lion's Club and the 40:8 Society.

Aurora University, Aurora, NJ   8/90-Present
Enrolled in courses toward a Bachelor Degree in Pre-Med/Health Science.

<table>
<tr><td></td><td align="center">**TERRA BEGGS**</td><td align="right">*COMBINATION*</td></tr>
</table>

1435 N.E. Sheridan Way
Boca Raton, FL 33432   407/555-8478

EXECUTIVE SECRETARY

PROFILE:

- Proven abilities in virtually all secretarial and administrative activities, including full responsibility for meetings, travel plans and special events.

- Skilled in shorthand, dictaphone, typing and correspondence writing, as well as WordPerfect and DisplayWrite IV; familiar with Lotus 1-2-3 and all types of general office equipment.

- Experience in total office management in absence of senior-level personnel; enjoy multiple tasks in fast-paced business environments, with personal, yet professional communication skills.

EMPLOYMENT:

House Mortgage Group, Miami, FL   7/92-12/92
Administrative Assistant to the President
Responsible for a wide range of office functions including correspondence writing/ distribution and professional telephone communications.
Organized travel itineraries and accommodations; purchased tickets, typed, filed and expedited messages and business schedules for the president.

Ant Hill Systems, Inc., Chicago, IL & Crawford, IN   9/87-5/92
Executive Secretary to the President & CEO
Organized a variety of functions for senior management of the corporate office and affiliates of this multi-divisional healthcare system.
Prioritized highly sensitive issues and events, including high-level meetings, calendars and business/personal travel plans.
Accurately typed all general and confidential correspondence.
* Promoted from: Executive Secretary to Chief Operating Officer & CFO; Executive Secretary to Vice President, Human Resources; Secretary to Corporate Director, Operations and Planning.

Anton's Union Station, Union, FL   4/86-9/87
Assistant Manager
Managed a 100-patron restaurant & lounge operation, including daily supervision and scheduling of wait staff.
Handled cost-effective purchasing of all food, beverages and supplies.

The Miami Road, Miami, FL   9/70-4/86
Administrative Assistant to the Vice President of Operations
Managed virtually all office functions and investigated freight damage claims with shippers and yard staff.
* Promoted from Secretary to Manager of Operations and Word Processing.

EDUCATION:

College of DuPage, Glendale, FL
Completed courses in office operations & computer systems.

ANNIE GREENSPRINGS   *COMBINATION*

630 Point Drive
Greenbrook, AL 60004   378/555-9816

MARKETING / ADVERTISING

EXPERIENCE:

- More than seven years in creative sales, marketing and advertising coordination, including full project management responsibilities.

- Design and expedite large-scale, multi-media marketing and promotional programs in major markets; organize all aspects of writing, graphic arts and production for printed materials.

- Experience in account prospecting and acquisition; plan and implement sales proposals; proficient in Windows, WordPerfect 5.1, Lotus and Microsoft Word for Macintosh.

- Handle job costing, budget development and forecasting; assist in cost-effective vendor sourcing; determine and meet specific client needs.

- Train and supervise sales and creative staff at virtually all levels of experience.

EMPLOYMENT: Purple Hills Country Club, Greenbrook, AL   3/92-Present
Marketing Coordinator
Assist the Food and Beverage Director in special projects, promotions and advertising for the F & B department, including the creative production and distribution of P.O.S. displays, newsletters, flyers, posters and direct mail pieces.

* Wrote, designed and printed an employee training manual.
* Work with banquet staff and coordinate food preparation and schedules for special events and parties.

SuperAds, Inc., Greenbrook, AL   3/88-1/92
Corporate Sales/Marketing Representative and Project Manager
Specialized in graphic design for displays: signage programs, barricades and window presentations.
Supervised up to 15 subcontractors in the coordination and production of large-scale, multi-media marketing programs.
Developed custom marketing strategies and media programs, involving design boards, copy writing/editing, keyline paste-up and transparencies.
Determined technical project specifications, i.e. cost, materials, placement, time and labor for the preparation of bids and proposals.
Handled scheduling of project fabrication and installation phases.
Utilized Lotus, WordPerfect, MS Word and Windows.
Gained experience in blueprint reading and interpretation.

* Top Sales Person for three years, with 90% repeat clients.
* Closed one of every three bids, with monthly sales up to $80,000.
* Designed and installed graphic displays for Sears Tower.
* Conducted research of current real estate projects and competitive products and services, with savings of up to 50% on specific projects.
* Determined and met specific client needs; conducted presentations and worked extensively with real estate developers, architects, designers and contractors in the use of graphic design for project promotion.

Japan Register Co., Northbrook, AL   8/85-3/88
Advertising Art / Marketing Coordinator
Supervised photographers and several projects simultaneously in the advertising department/print communications division.
Coordinated artwork and production for a 1,500-page annual catalog, direct mail flyers and brochures for hotels and resorts worldwide.
Provided direct, creative input to vendors regarding artwork and copy for specific projects.

Assisted in photo styling, package design, layout, editing, proofreading and paste-up.
Specified typestyles, copy sizes, colors and placement of printed materials.
Supervised press checks; operated a stat camera and scaled transparencies.

* Maintained positive communications with purchasing staff and merchandise buyers.
* Acted as corporate representative at numerous industry trade shows.

EDUCATION: University of San Francisco, San Francisco, CA
                    B.A. Degree - Art, Design Emphasis   1984
                    Minor: Art History

INTERNSHIPS: San Francisco Museum of Art   1984
                    Assistant Director: Coordinated all aspects of exhibits and programs.

                    University of San Diego   1982
                    Alumni Coordinator: Coordinated and planned alumni events; operated a computer for data entry related to former and future alumni.

                    Midco International   Summers, 1980-1981
                    Art Director / Assistant: Performed layout and keyline paste-up of brochures for a restaurant equipment company.

LEWIS PETERS   *COMBINATION*

2185 Short-End Circle
Streamwood, IN 30172   689/555-4059

TELECOMMUNICATIONS ANALYST

A technical position where skills in supervision or management can contribute to the overall profitability of a growing company.

PROFILE:

- More than ten years in telecommunications and computer operations, including responsibility for multishift functions and complete hub planning and management.

- Effectively hire, train and supervise technical staff in system repair and database updating; determine & solve hardware, circuit and software problems.

- Experience in full system design, installation, analysis and troubleshooting for E-mail, file transfers, large database networks and wide area networks.

- Knowledge of high-speed data links and all levels of multiplexing, as well as full documentation of network management systems and modems.

- Utilize and maintain synchronous/asynchronous transmissions over various networks; skilled in Xerox systems, CODEX 6040 multiplexers and the 9800 network management system; experience with a wide range of mainframes and peripherals.

CAREER BACKGROUND:

Amoco Corporation, Roselle, IN   8/88-Present
Telecommunication Technician
Perform second-level troubleshooting and analysis for telecommunication systems handling large volumes of data from Amoco offices and refineries worldwide.
Communicate with virtually all levels of Amoco personnel to maintain system viability for E-mail, file transfers and a major database.
* Successfully directed the installation of Amoco's first network management system for analog circuits, a CODEX 9800.
* Utilize an SNA network-X.25, microwave networks and a T-1 backbone.

Canon Corporation, Park Ridge and Des Plaines, IN   4/73-8/88
Technical Support Manager   2/85-8/88
Planned and implemented procedures for the support of 450 users; managed an entire equipment room for the Field Service Organization.
Directed two technical specialists and an information systems coordinator; conducted staff career counseling and performance reviews.
Handled troubleshooting of Honeywell and Raytheon terminals and controllers, as well as Codex modems and ATTIS DSUs; tested coax cables for continuity.
* Coordinated equipment moves and installs with end users and electricians; tracked and resolved circuit related problems.

* Installed and maintained a Xerox Ethernet system and managed an inventory of all related equipment and circuits.
* Ensured accurate documentation and operational procedures, as well as environmental stability.
* Attended monthly planning sessions with users and senior-level staff.

Operations Manager   3/83-2/85

Managed a three-shift batch processing and telecommunications operation using a Xerox Sigma 6 mainframe with CP-V software, a multi-tape drive, disk drive and high-speed printers.

Maintained a high level of user service on a base of three Honeywell level 6 computers using GCOS/TPS software.

Provided a technical interface with vendors for documentation, safety/security and tape library audits.

* Conducted staff training, career planning and performance reviews.
* Responsible for expense controls related to overtime and supplies.
* During installation of an HP 3000/68, coordinated operations training and developed operational guidelines to support the parts warehouse.
* Organized the shutdown and removal of computer room equipment at the end of batch operations.

Senior Computer Operator / Schedule Planner   2/79-3/83

Developed run-time schedules, technical support and daily monitoring of computer room activities for three shifts.

Performed JCL modifications, disk contention and batch processing analysis.

Updated documentation and schedules for critical tape transmissions and quality control.

* Analyzed and developed the process for enhancing batch processing through-put and minimized reruns.
* Earned the Xerox "Praise Award" for outstanding achievement.

Computer Operator Trainee / Computer Operator   4/73-2/79

Responsible for batch and telecommunications processing on three shifts.

* Consistently met critical transmission and report schedules and documented all hardware errors and operational problems.

EDUCATION: Amoco Corporation: Completed various company courses including: PCP Network Operations, CLI & Telematics Directory Structure, PCP Hardware Installation and Maintenance, Performance Management, ISDN Protocols and DR2D Radio Maintenance.

Xerox: Attended the Management Studies Program.
AMI: Completed *Supervisory Skills* and *Working With People*.

Oakton Community College: Courses included Human Behavior.
DePaul University: Enrolled in the School for New Learning toward a B.A. in Telecommunications.

RICHARD E. TILAN   COMBINATION
625 Edwards Lane
Streamwood, AK 60107   312/555-5079

CONSTRUCTION / BUILDING MANAGEMENT

BACKGROUND:
- Successful experience in the management of virtually all building construction/upgrade activities from concept to completion.

- Supervise quality control and adherence to specifications by architects, engineers, developers and tradesmen; work directly with local building officials; proficient in blueprint development/interpretation.

- Handle full budget development and implementation; organize subcontractors and ensure cost-effective materials purchasing; negotiate labor and material contracts in a professional manner.

- Coordinate major projects including bid preparation/analysis for parking lots, masonry, plumbing, H.V.A.C., electrical, fixtures and roofing.

EXPERIENCE:
Sears Roebuck & Co., Chicago, IL and locations nationwide   1971-7/94
PROJECT MANAGER   1986-7/94

In charge of all construction operations and fixturing for several new and existing Ward stores throughout the U.S., with projects ranging up to $10 million.

Responsible for all building construction, maintenance and repair expenditures.

Analyze/troubleshoot problems and supervise activities; provide financial/status reports, as well as full documentation of labor, materials and project specifications.

Write and present proposals for new retail store construction and the upgrading of existing buildings including:

1994 Projects in Illinois:
New Stores: St. Charles, $2.3 million; Crestwood, $1.5m. Remodelings: Vernon Hills, $250k; Oak Brook, new entrances, $600k; Chicago Ridge, $550k.

Involved in specification review and proposal development for the following projects until approval of contract:
Merrillville, IN, $320k repaving; Orland Park, IL, $480k repaving; Saginaw, MI, $710k repaving; Toledo, OH, $514k repaving; Joliet, IL, $600k repaving; Cedar Rapids, IA, $640k repaving; Fairview Hts, IL, $550k reroofing; Des Moines, IA, $150k masonry restoration.

Project Administrator for the first 50 percent of construction of new stores in:
Midland, MI, $1.7m; Rochester, MN, $2.5m; Marion, IL, $2.8m.

Directed the successful completion and cost-effectiveness for the following maintenance projects on retail stores, 1990:
St. Louis, MO, $250k masonry restoration; W. Lafayette, IN, $330k reroofing; Pontiac, MI, $486k reroofing; Schaumburg, IL, $980k reroofing.

Managed all aspects of construction for the following new stores, 1990:
Irondequoit, NY, $6.4m; Manchester, CT, $8.9m; Bay City, MI, $2m; Coon Rapids, MN, $1.5m; Bradley-Northfield, IL, $2.9m; Danville, IL, $1.6m.

Project Manager for new stores in 1989:
Buffalo, NY, $3.3m; Ithaca, NY, $1.5m; N. Attleboro, MA, $9.5m; Kingston, NY, $3.3m; Kingston, MA, $1.9m.

Remodeling/improvement projects, 1989:
Saugus, MA, $470k new air conditioner & chiller; L. Grove, NY, $450k reroofing, masonry restoration & new entrances; New Brunswick, NJ, $990k reroofing; Hackensack, NJ, $173k reroofing; Merrillville, IN, $398k repaving; Warwick, RI, $700k reroofing; Albany, NY, $1.6m reroofing & masonry restoration.

TERRITORIAL FIXTURING SUPERINTENDENT   1983-1985

Directed the completion of up to $5m in store retrofit and fixturing projects, including all phases of merchandising.
Simultaneously coordinated up to 80 tradesmen and Ward personnel; ensured conformance to budgets and time parameters.
Supervised all union tradesmen including Installers, Fire Protection Staff, Mechanical Installers, Electricians, Carpenters, Painters and Carpet Installers.

- Maintained records for all monies and projects and approved additional work as required.
- Analyzed/approved competitive bids from numerous trades.
- Coordinated the installation of a concessions, including facilities for optical department, financial network, photo departments and beauty salons.

*** Excellent track record of completing major store fixturings in 1983, 1984 and 1985 on time and under budget.

PLANNING SUPERVISOR   1981-1983

Reroofing and Masonry Restoration, Existing Wards Facilities.
Successfully managed up to $12 million/year in restoration projects, including researching new construction methods, products and specific job/quality criteria.
Performed inspections of established Ward units; evaluated problems and recommended corrective measures to store and warehouse management.
Assembled and prepared accurate cost estimates; developed formal write-ups and bidders' lists for company approval.

CHIEF PLANNER   1971-1981

A full range of sales support activities included drafting and the planning/remodeling of auto centers, service centers, convenience and distribution centers, credit centrals and catalog/telephone sales & stockrooms.
Supervised fixturing changes for merchandising trends through staff communications.

WILLIAM A. BRYERS, CPA

22136 South Juniper Avenue

Louis, IL 70067

431/555-9538

COMBINATION

OBJECTIVE: A position as Corporate Controller or Manager, where analytical and leadership skills would contribute to a firm's bottom-line profitability.

PROFILE:
- Comprehensive skills in accounting system design and management, including responsibility for staff coordination, financial reporting, audits and reviews.

- Effectively train and supervise accounting staff in full ledger maintenance, billing, AP/AR and payroll procedures.

- Proficient in Lotus 1-2-3 and various general ledger packages for spreadsheet development and data compilation; handle all aspects of federal and state tax planning and preparation for large and small corporations.

CAREER BACKGROUND:

Masters & Johnson, CPAs, Louis, IL   8/87-6/95
MANAGER
Responsible for up to six certified audits and numerous reviews and/or compilations at a wide range of companies on an annual basis.
Trained and supervised up to three professionals per project; determined and met specific client needs for complete ledger maintenance and reporting.
Improved client systems and procedures to ensure strong internal controls.
Processed/reviewed federal and state individual and corporate tax returns.
* Manage complete accounting projects for firms with up to $277 million in annual sales.
* Maintain an up-to-date knowledge of current federal and state tax codes.

Cobain and Morrison, CPAs, Oak Brook, IL   11/85-7/87
CERTIFIED PUBLIC ACCOUNTANT
Performed accounting services for tax returns and real estate partnerships.
Distributed K-1s and updated/reported journal entries of year-end activity.
Prepared projections and forecasts for rental properties.

Rogers & Akron, CPAs, Palatine, IL   11/81-11/85
SENIOR ACCOUNTANT
Handled all public accounting duties at numerous companies, including all federal and state tax preparation.

Chetham & Howe CPAs, Chicago, IL   12/79-10/81
JUNIOR ACCOUNTANT
Responsibilities included write-up work, audit assistance and tax preparation.

EDUCATION: DePaul University, School of Commerce, Chicago, IL   Graduated 1979
               B.S. Degree, Accounting Major   * Dean's List

               Wright Jr. College, Chicago, IL   Graduated 1976
               A.S. Degree, Graduated with Honors

SUSAN PAINTER
23 Rue de Coleur
Westmont, NM 40559
854/555-5260

COMBINATION

ART GALLERY ADMINISTRATION

A position requiring creativity and innovation, as well as technical knowledge in the creative arts.

THUMBNAIL SKETCH:

- ♦ Experience in curating and contributing original work to numerous Fine Art exhibitions in the Westmont area.

- ♦ Creative talents in various art mediums, including monotypes, pastels and acrylic & oil painting.

- ♦ Communicate well with artists and dealers; handle customer relations in high-pressure situations; familiar with WordStar and Lotus 1-2-3 for correspondence writing and general bookkeeping.

CAREER EXPERIENCE:

Dali's House, Westmont, NM   1/90-Present
Receptionist / General Office Facilitator
Responsible for direct client relations on a daily basis, which involves sales, scheduling inquiries and writing correspondence.
Performed gallery advertising and promotion through direct mailings and telemarketing.
Updated and maintained client files on a PC with Wordstar.

→   Increased total sales volume over two years by 20 percent.

Green Planet Shops, Westmont, NM   Part-time, 1/90-6/92
Sales Associate
Conducted sales presentations in a professional manner.
Managed and coordinated merchandise inventory and prepared semiannual inventory reports using Lotus 1-2-3.
Trained new personnel in sales and the marketing of merchandise through in-store customer contact and advertising flyers.

University of Arizona Art Gallery, Tempe, AZ   1987-1989
Gallery Assistant
Assisted in curating major art shows on-campus.
Ensured prompt delivery, layout and installation of artwork.
Provided receptionist services and answered telephone inquiries during art shows and regular viewing hours.

→   Coordinated art show schedules and distribution of original advertising.

<u>Jemster Gallery,</u> Westchester, NM   Summer, 1988
Receptionist / General Office Facilitator
Responsible for the creative installation of new artwork.
Maintained client files and purchase records using a PC and Lotus 1-2-3.

ART SHOWS: <u>Cousin's College,</u> Chicago, IL   5/92
Curated a Senior Art Show, including the selection, organization and installation of 15 pieces.

<u>Calabrese College,</u> Manhattan, NY   5/92
One original acrylic painting on display.

<u>NO WAY OUT Cafe and Gallery,</u> Los Angeles, CA   4/92
Curated a personal art show with eight pieces, including paintings and monotypes.

<u>River North Cafe,</u> Chicago, IL   2/92
Contributed three monotypes to a group art show.

<u>Avalon,</u> Chicago, IL   2/91
Participated in a group art show with seven other artists and contributed mixed media pieces.

<u>Diva Cafe,</u> Darien, NM   12/90-2/91
Curated a personal art show with 12 pieces on display, including drawings and acrylic paintings.

<u>Columbia College,</u> Chicago, IL   6/90
Participated in a student art show with two paintings.

<u>College of DuPage,</u> Glen Ellyn, IL   6/89
Participated in a student art show with one pastel.

<u>College of DuPage Gallery,</u> Glen Ellyn, IL   1987
Displayed a drawing and a photograph in a student art show.

EDUCATION: <u>Columbia College,</u> Chicago, IL   1990-1992
B.A. Degree, Fine Arts

→   Maintained a full course load while working 25 hours per week.

<u>College of DuPage,</u> Glen Ellyn, IL   1986-1989
Completed course work toward Fine Arts degree.

RONALD W. CAMPBELL

COMBINATION

1491 Foxboro Court
Addison, AK 52107

438/555-0792

PHARMACEUTICAL / MEDICAL SUPPLY SALES

EXPERIENCE:

▸ More than five years in medical product sales, marketing and strategic planning, including full responsibility for account prospecting and management.

▸ Plan and conduct detailed product presentations for medical staff at all levels of experience; excellent knowledge of cardiovascular and antibiotic medications; skilled in new product introduction and marketing.

▸ Experience with hospital formularies; handle pricing, negotiations and all aspects of contract administration.

EMPLOYMENT:

Searle Pharmaceutical, Spring House, AK — 1/87-Present
Sales Representative — 4/89-Present
Responsible for selling various types of pharmaceuticals to hospital and office-based physicians and pharmacies in a Chicagoland territory.
Conduct detailed product presentations, following full product research.
Manage more than 300 accounts including six hospitals, three of which are teaching hospitals.
Responsible for all aspects of product distribution and account tracking on a PC; compile & present reports on product samples, inventories and account activity.
Handle full account troubleshooting and timely call-backs.

* Plan and conduct Continuing Medical Education (CME) accredited in-service programs for all types of medical personnel.
* Personally acquired two teaching hospital accounts.
* Contender for the Stratosphere award, given for the highest market shares and change in share on promoted products within each region, 1990.
* Earned Regional Sales Award for top district sales in the region, 1989.

Corporate Representative — 1/87-4/89
* Earned Sales Training Achievement Recognition (S.T.A.R.) for outstanding first year performance, including proficiency in product lines, sales skills, territory management and sales performance.

Sherwin Williams Company, Cleveland, OH — 2/84-1/87
Manager
Performed marketing and sales to wholesale accounts.
Hired, trained and supervised sales personnel; processed credits and collections.
Promoted to this position from Operations Manager with a crew of 14.
Responsible for billing, inventory control, credit and store operations.

EDUCATION:

University of Illinois at Chicago, IL
Bachelor of Arts Degree: Economics — 8/83

JACQUELINE A. SAILOR   *COMBINATION*

2227 Land's End
Gorda, IL 60193   708/555-6306

OBJECTIVE:	A position in the Travel Industry, where more than nine years in customer and technical services would be of value.

ABILITIES:
- ▸ Experience in full travel expediting: ticketing, baggage supervision, pilot and aircraft scheduling and priority shipping; skilled in SABRE and SONIC reservation systems.

- ▸ Train and supervise staff in company procedures, customer relations and problem solving in high-pressure situations.

EXPERIENCE:

<u>United Airlines,</u> Chicago, IL   1989-Present
Service Agent
In charge of a full range of baggage services including investigation, tracing and reporting of lost or damaged items, as well as processing of financial settlements.
Handle daily preparation of written reports and data entry/retrieval using SABRE.
Manage five employees as night supervisor and facilitate package routing.
*   Completed extensive training in Customer Relations.

<u>Iranian Airways,</u> Chicago, IL   1985-1989
Trainer / Customer Service Representative
Responsible for all aspects of ticketing including check-ins, boarding/gate operations and transaction reporting.
Trained new employees in all areas of customer relations at various sites.
*   Gained a working knowledge of SABRE and SONIC reservation systems.

<u>Dayton Greyhound Park,</u> Dubuque, IA   1985-1986
Customer Service Agent / Financial Clerk
Assisted in daily reporting, data entry/retrieval and general ledger preparation.

<u>South Central Airlines,</u> Dubuque, IA   1982-1984
Customer Service Agent / Flight Controller
Handled all areas of customer relations, including ticketing, baggage investigation and claim settlement.
Coordinated crew and aircraft scheduling and maintenance; assisted in payroll processing and disbursement.

EDUCATION:

<u>McConnell School - "20" Course,</u> Minneapolis, MN   1982
Trained in airline travel procedures

<u>Northeast Iowa Technical Institute,</u> Dubuque, IA   1981
Certified Activity Coordinator

<table>
<tr><td></td><td>**MELISSA BOSKEY**</td><td>*COMBINATION*</td></tr>
</table>

301 Water Street
St. Charles, IL 63147   414/555-0446

OBJECTIVE: *FINANCE / MANAGEMENT*
A position where interpersonal skills, technical expertise and leadership talents would be utilized.

PROFILE:
- Executive-level talents in the direction and streamlining of corporate financial operations, including full responsibility for financial reporting and cost reduction.

- Consistently plan, implement and improve systems for product costing, internal control, special projects and all general accounting; interface with bankers and attorneys to coordinate financing arrangements and monitor debt compliance.

- Proficient in budget administration and variance analyses; work closely with senior-level executives in procedure planning and the monitoring of business operations.

- Effectively hire, train and supervise staff in audits, monthly/annual reporting and SEC compliance, including 10K, 10Q and registration statements.

CAREER BACKGROUND: Craig Financial Services, Schaumburg, IL
Craig Financial Services is a nationwide specialty insurance underwriter, marketer and provider of managed health care services.

Vice President of Finance   9/93-Present
Manage a full range of finance and accounting operations, including coordination of extensive research, variance analyses and reporting for business monitoring.
Administer several budgets and approve significant capital expenditures.
Hire, train and supervise 10 employees in monthly statement preparation, accounts payable/receivable and invoicing for three subsidiaries.
Interface with account service and sales reps, as well as marketing, human resource and legal departments to monitor all business-related activities.
Utilize Lotus 1-2-3 and WordPerfect.

* Developed and implemented a new system for product costing.
* Analyzed and reduced expenses by 15%, including labor and facility costs.
* Monitor debt compliance.
* Perform/oversee the updating of accounting procedure manuals.

First Vice President   6/90-9/93
Managed daily operations of the noninsurance accounting department.
Responsible for SEC compliance, including 10Ks, 10Qs and filings related to debt and stock offerings; coordinated with auditors and legal counsel.
Directed bank covenant and compliance testing.

* Compiled and presented data for annual reports to stockholders.

Melissa Boskey   **Page Two**

Controller   6/89-6/90
In charge of all noninsurance subsidiaries and the reorganization of all accounting procedures.
Trained and supervised staff in the preparation of all noninsurance financial statements for senior-level management.
Initiated more effective and accurate procedures, including variance analyses, internal controls and the monitoring of cash flow requirements.

* Managed and improved consolidations for this company's operation.

Arthur Andersen, Chicago, IL
Senior Accountant   4/87-4/89
Effectively trained and supervised up to five accountants in audits for construction, financial and manufacturing clients.
Evaluated and documented internal controls; prepared and analyzed financial statements, including internal control recommendations.
Planned/reviewed audit staff procedures, which included budget monitoring and staff recruitment.
Conducted inventory analyses, cost build-ups, standard development and price testing.
Utilized various inventory costing methodologies for several manufacturing clients.
Analyzed foreign currency transactions for an international client.

* Promoted from Staff Accountant, 6/84-4/87.
* Performed SEC filings and consolidations; reviewed annual reports, income statements, balance sheets, footnotes and letters of opinion.
* Prepared staff performance evaluations and recommended advancements.
* Utilized Lotus 1-2-3 and WordPerfect.

EDUCATION: Southern Illinois University, Carbondale, IL

                  M.B.A. Degree, Executive MBA program   Graduated 5/93

                  B.S. Degree, Accounting   Graduated 5/84

CERTIFICATION: Certified Public Accountant, State of Illinois. Passed first sitting, 5/84.

MEMBERSHIPS: Illinois CPA Society and the AICPA.

RUSSELL W. BIRD, JR.

COMBINATION

224 Aspen Place
Austin, TX 50173

345/555-8104

EXPERIENCE:

- Hands-on experience in production, supervision and quality control, with a thorough knowledge of Mazak and Heidelberg machine centers.

- Skilled tool maker and machinist; quickly adapt to new systems, procedures and product lines.

- Familiar with engineering designs and product theory; interface with production, management and engineering staff at all levels of experience.

- Skilled in Computerized Numerical Control, SPC inspection and blueprint reading; utilize precision hand tools and measuring instruments.

EMPLOYMENT:

Better Stuff Molds, Inc., Austin, TX   1990-Present
TOOL MACHINIST
Responsible for machine operations and quality assurance in the production of mold bases and plastic components.
Interface with CNC programmers and participate in SPC efforts.
Work directly with engineers and provide input regarding machinery and practical equipment applications.

→ Leader of the Safety Board Committee; planned and implemented numerous plant safety procedures.

Dynamo Grinders, Cleveland, OH   1978-1990
LEAD MACHINIST
Supervised and scheduled up to 12 employees in the precision manufacture of hydraulic and pneumatic valves.
Oversaw the CNC department and coordinated SPC quality assurance inspections.
Participated in production planning with senior-level personnel.

→ Consistently met or exceeded the highest standards of quality for a demanding customer base.
→ Completed company sponsored training in Quality Control, SPC and Blueprint Reading.

EDUCATION:

University of Akron, Akron, OH
Completed numerous courses toward a B.S. in Manufacturing Technology.

LINDA DAVESTER   *COMBINATION*

1124 Horace Lane
Winslow, NC 40110   658/555-3597

CREDIT / COLLECTIONS REPRESENTATIVE

PROFILE:

♦ More than nine years in the analysis of loans and credit/collection operations, including full responsibility for payment plans, rate negotiations and customer service.

♦ Assist in training and supervising staff in professional credit and collection operations: credit checks, transaction processing/reporting and currency conversions.

♦ Establish credit limits and update & maintain client accounts on computer systems; familiar with Lotus 1-2-3, CDI software and the AT&T 705.

CAREER BACKGROUND:

Faster Flying Service, Wood Dale, NC   4/90-Present
Accounts Receivable Supervisor
Responsible for collections, credit policies, customer service and hundreds of accounts for this air freight transportation service.
Assist in supervising up to 16 employees in journal entries and compiling/ presenting monthly status reports.
Interface with branch office managers to resolve accounting issues and problems.
* Work extensively with "hard core" collections on a regular basis.
* Distribute cash on customer accounts and mediate disputed accounts.
* Prepare daily bank deposits and report directly to management.

Venus Electric Corporation, Crystal Lake, NC   3/87-8/89
Credit and Collections Specialist, International Operations Div.   3/89-8/89
Updated, maintained and distributed customer accounts on a daily basis, including the processing of incoming receivables for the international division.
Initiated and performed credit checks; established credit histories and authorized tracing of overdue drafts and/or letters of credit.
* Monitored day-to-day exchange rates for foreign currency conversions.
* Calculated percentages of commissions paid to distributors.
* Compiled and presented monthly statements of pre-established distributors and customers for their reviews.
* Promoted to this position from **Administrative Secretary** and **Commission Administrator.**

General Mills Company / Stuart Laboratories, Barrington, NC   8/82-12/85
Serial Publication and Information Librarian

EDUCATION: Central YMCA Community College
Major: Business Administration; Career Major: Business Law

RALPH PREWICK   *COMBINATION*

2720 Berry Street
Norridge, UT 43657   679/555-2234

OBJECTIVE: ***DESIGN ENGINEERING***
A position where proven skills in CAD/CAM systems, preferably related to new products and business environments.

PROFILE:
- More than seven years in virtually all aspects of product design, development, production and inspection on CAD/CAM systems.

- Assist in staff training and supervision in 2-D & 3-D design and drafting; assign/organize work and interface with technical staff and engineers in a professional manner.

- Utilize 3-D finite element analysis and solids modeling; skilled in IBM CAD-PAK, SuperLaunch and CADAM systems.

EMPLOYMENT: Sparrow-Hoffman Corp., Cylinder Division, Norridge, UT   1987-Present
Design Engineer, CAD/CAM Systems
Perform product design and development for this major manufacturer of cylinders, pistons, rods and all types of hydraulic and pneumatic equipment.
Train and supervise up to five employees.
Responsible for work scheduling, assignments and special projects.
Assist in all development functions for parts and finished products.

▸ Work extensively with R&D personnel for new CAD/CAM designs.

Robert Morris College, Salt Lake City, UT   1985-1987
Teacher's Assistant
Instructed students in drafting and design techniques.
Performed CAD-PAK 2-D drafting, BRAVO 2 & 3-D design, drafting, solids modeling and finite element analysis.
Tracked individual student performance; administered tests and answered technical questions.

EDUCATION: Utah University, Calumet, UT   Expected Graduation: 1993
B.S. Degree: Mechanical Engineering

Salt Shaker College, Salt Lake City, UT
A.S. Degree: Pre-Engineering   Graduated 1987

▸ Completed extensive training in CADAM, BRAVO and CAD-PAK systems.

COREY J. APPLE   *FUNCTIONAL*

678 Norridge Lane
Addison, MD 50101   768/555-1260

OBJECTIVE:	***Aircraft Mechanic / Pilot*** A position where demonstrated flying skills and/or mechanical expertise would be utilized.

PROFILE:

- Licensed as Private Pilot, single and multiengine land/instrument planes, Commercial Pilot, Airframe Mechanic, Power Plant Mechanic and Certified Flight Instructor.

- Experience in flying instruction, including experience with the Cessna 150, 152, 172, 172RG, Piper Warrior, Piper Aztec and Turbo Arrow.

- Skilled in the use of lathes and standard shop equipment, as well as:

  → Weighing & balancing of control surfaces
  → Removal & replacement of skin panels & aircraft fasteners
  → Manufacture and testing of control cables
  → Comprehensive modification of aircraft structures
  → Corrosion control and aircraft painting
  → Power shears, band saws and the Conrac Synchrobender
  → Erco sheet metal formers and the Di-Arco turret punch
  → Hand and power rollers, belt sanders, drill presses, lathes & mills

EDUCATION:

Northern Maryland University, Carbondale, MD
Bachelor of Science Degree -- Aviation Management   12/92
Associate Degree -- Aviation Maintenance   8/92
Associate Degree -- Applied Sciences   8/90

→ Overall GPA: 3.0/4.0

EMPLOYMENT:

Self-funded college costs through employment at:

Blue Jay Construction Company, Bloomingdale, MD
Apprentice   Summers/Breaks, 1990-Present
Responsible for electrical, plumbing and carpentry work on office buildings, townhomes, single family homes and warehouses.

Ronnie's Office Furniture Warehouse, Itasca, MD   Summers, 1988-1989
Forklift Driver / Order Puller

Federal Express, Addison, MD   1/86-7/87
Customer Service Representative
Performed shipping/receiving and truck loading & unloading on a daily basis.

MORRIE NIECE

COMBINATION

2262 Lincoln Street
Hanover Park, IL 60126

708/555-6114

PRINTING OPERATIONS / MANAGEMENT

BACKGROUND:

- Skilled in hiring, training and supervising press workers in makeready and quality control; work closely with customers in full project troubleshooting.

- Proven abilities in virtually all aspects of printing, including full responsibility for press configuration, setup and teardown.

- Perform color matching, registration and full press maintenance; experience with 4- 5- and 6-color web presses up to 38" including:

  ▸ Harris M-1000 4-color web & sheeter *and* 6-color web with sheeter, double former folder and combination folder
  ▸ Harris M-110 4-color web with in-line finishing and sheeter
  ▸ Hantsho 4-color web with in-line finishing & sheeter and 2-color w/sheeter
  ▸ Didde Glaser 4-color web with in-line finishing and sheeter
  ▸ Baker Perkins C-14 4-color web with in-line finishing and sheeter

EMPLOYMENT:

Blue Sky Poster, Elk Grove Village, IL   7/88-12/94
Pressman
Handled a wide range of printing projects on the Harris 6-color press, including direct customer service and problem solving on a daily basis.
Trained and supervised one pressman and two feeders in all operations.

Technical Sources, Wheeling, IL   1983-1988
Foreman
Responsible for the operation of seven presses, with sheeter and in-line finishing. Worked closely with all customers and promptly resolved problems with quality and turnaround time.
  ▸ Handled final approval of color quality.
  ▸ Trained and supervised up to 40 employees.

Worldwide Web Company, Itasca, IL   1982-1983
Pressman
Duties included full makeready, color and register setup.
Communicated daily with customers regarding special projects and quality.

Vessel Printing Co., Elk Grove Village, IL   1973-1982
First Pressman and Feeder

EDUCATION:

High School Graduate

MILITARY:

U.S. Army Veteran   **Sergeant, E-5**

TONY SPAVONE
2277 Homer Drive
Springfield, IL 60108

COMBINATION

708/555-6370

EQUIPMENT MAINTENANCE / REPAIR
A position utilizing proven abilities in production equipment repair and operation.

EXPERIENCE:

♦ More than four years in the repair and maintenance of manufacturing equipment, including various robotic and packaging systems.

♦ Assist in production staff training and performance tracking; handle system streamlining and cost reduction with staff and supervisors.

♦ Skilled in a wide range of packing and wrapping machinery, including Bosch Baggers, Ishida Scales, MOE Lidders, Douglas APVs and various cutters and gluers.

♦ Handle changeovers and preventive maintenance; trained in OSHA and quality control standards, as well as plant safety and documentation.

EMPLOYMENT:

Snicker Town, Chicago, IL   1989-Present
Troubleshooter / Operator
Responsible for the repair, maintenance and fine-tuning of timing belts, conveyors and gear boxes on all wrapping and packing equipment.
Handle troubleshooting malfunctions and route repair requests to appropriate departments.
Enter and update work orders on the corporate MIS system.
Perform gear box adjustments and fine tuning.
Conduct changeovers and repairs with a minimum of downtime.
Attend in-house basic and advanced courses; completed a corporate program on Quality Assurance procedures.
Install lockouts on machinery to prevent unauthorized use and accidents.

* Preventive maintenance duties include lubrication of moving parts, cleaning/regreasing cams, scale and robot calibration, belt welding, rebuilding or replacement, glue system flushing and nextday setups.
* Train employees in basic tool use and review worker performance for supervisors.
* Completed extensive weekend training as Packer for six months.

Lance General Hospital, Park Ridge, IL   Part-time: 1986-1989
Food Service Technician
Prepared patient food trays according to dietary needs and physicians' orders.
Delivered meals to patient floors.

EDUCATION:

Elgin Community College, Elgin, IL
Certificate: Machine Technology   4/89
Trained in Jigs & Fixtures, Blueprint Reading, Autocad CAD/CAM, Die Design and Mathematics.

JAMES D. RISE

COMBINATION

2213 Mammon Avenue
DePaul, OH 40123

443/555-4478

OBJECTIVE:	***MORTGAGE BANKING*** A position where executive-level skills would be utilized.

PROFILE:

- More than nine years in management and mortgage banking, including full responsibility for department operations.

- Coordinate all related documentation and services with attorneys, trustees and investors.

- Effectively hire, train and supervise staff in the monitoring of portfolio and inventory REOs, foreclosures and bankruptcies on automated systems.

- Coordinate the timely filing of foreclosure claims with the FHA/VA and PMI, as well as compliance with FREDDIE MAC, FNMA and private investors.

EMPLOYMENT:

<u>Slip & Loan Mortgage, Inc.</u>, Dayton, OH   2/84-5/92
Assistant Vice President - Mortgage Disposition   12/90-5/92
Responsible for seven employees and all MD department operations, including customer service and the monitoring of up to 450 bankruptcies and 250 loans in the foreclosure and claims areas.
Work with attorneys and agencies listed above for prompt, efficient service.
Ensure delivery of default letters; review new filings for possible cramdown characteristics.

- *   Reviewed all monthly status reports for accuracy.
- *   Coordinate staff and attorneys in the determination and resolution of specific client problems.
- *   Plan and implement strategies for loss reduction and professional customer service.
- *   Promoted to this position from:

Assistant Vice President, Collections
Managed collection procedures for a portfolio of 50,000 loans, with an emphasis on FHA/VA loans.
Hired, trained and supervised more than 15 employees in all operations and conducted their performance reviews.
Analyzed/reviewed all files prior to submission to the foreclosure review board.
Ensured compliance with FREDDIE MAC, FNMA and private investor requirements; maintained accuracy of monthly reports sent to all investors.

Assistant Manager, Escrow Department
Responsible for hiring, training and managing 20 employees in hazard insurance claim processing.
Consistently reviewed and improved procedures & operations.

Special Task Force: Assistant to the President
Responsible for troubleshooting of receivables, MIP open items and PMI open items.

Southern Dairy Corporation, Elgin, OH   1979-1984
Machine Operator
Operated plastic injection molding and filling machines in a safe, cost-effective manner.

Machined Products, Elgin, OH   1976-1979
Plant Manager
In charge of all plant operations and the training and supervision of up to 15 employees.
Performed cost-effective purchasing, inventory control, shipping and distribution.

EDUCATION: The Mortgage Banking Association
                               Earned Certificate for completion of various courses in mortgage banking.

                               T. Frank Hardesty Seminar:
                               The Art of Managing Collections

                               Saint Edwards High School, Elgin, OH   Graduated 1963

STEVEN B. TIRED   *COMBINATION*

2653 Catalpa Lane
Bartlett, MI 40103   673/555-0798

OBJECTIVE: **SOLID / HAZARDOUS WASTE MANAGEMENT**
A position where hands-on training would be utilized.

PROFILE:

- Proven abilities in research and material/cost estimating; trained in biomonitoring system design and analysis; familiar with RCRA and CERCLA legislation.

- Handle written & oral communications in a professional manner; strong aptitude for learning technical systems and procedures.

- Familiar with Lotus 1-2-3 and Quattro for spreadsheets, as well as WordStar and WordPerfect 5.1.

EMPLOYMENT: <u>Village of Bartlett,</u> Bartlett, MI   Summer, 1991
Internship
Assisted in material and cost estimating for several village projects.
Responsible for collecting measurements of sidewalks and streets and updating all documentation.
Involved in setting slopes at construction sites.
Collected data and handled plan reviews, as well as a variety of field work.
Communicated with city residents and resolved problems and complaints.

<u>American Flange,</u> Carol Stream, MI   Summers
Materials Handler

<u>Builders Square</u> and <u>Walgreens,</u> Bartlett, MI   School Breaks & Summers
Cashier / Customer Service Representative

EDUCATION: <u>University of Illinois,</u> Urbana-Champaign, IL
Bachelor of Science Degree   May, 1992
Major: Civil Engineering   **Concentration: Environmental Engineering**

- * Major GPA: 4.3/5.0
- * Self-funded 100 percent of college costs.
- * Class projects included extensive research and the writing of a 20-page report on surface drainage of an urban creek.
- * Key courses included:
  Wastewater Management, Air & Water Quality Control
  Solid and Hazardous Waste Management and Biomonitoring

JEROME TISHKA   *COMBINATION*

7732 Box Elder Lane
Golden, CO 60107
338/555-4894

OBJECTIVE: **SYSTEM ANALYST / PROGRAMMER**
A position in a PC environment, where diverse technical skills would be utilized.

PROFILE:

- Skilled in application programming, system design and support for a variety of businesses through a data processing service bureau.

- Experience with hardware including the ES 9000, the 4300 series, S/370 model 135, S/360 models 30 & 40 and the Nixdorf system 680; fluent in IBM Assembler (ALC); familiar with COBOL, RPG and DOS/VS.

- Perform manual/computer conversions, as well as staff supervision and the writing of detailed accounting applications.

CAREER EXPERIENCE:

Sybase Corporation, Park Ridge, CO   1965-4/95
Production Support Analyst   1990-4/95
Responsible for the design, writing and maintenance of all programs for numerous businesses, including troubleshooting and debugging.
Applications included accounts payable/receivable, payroll, order entry, inventory control, sales analysis, cost analysis, "Fix It" and various conversion programs.
Programmed and maintained the AT&T system 75 telephone system.
Performed troubleshooting of programs distributed by the national support center; handled program changes, adds and deletions.

* Utilized hardware and languages listed above, as well as the IBM 1401 and CDC BackLash 480.
* Produced over 220 programs on IBM systems.
* Promoted to this position from:

Associate Project Analyst
Performed system design and handled extensive customer relations and problem solving in a professional manner.

Programmer Analyst
Designed and wrote a wide range of application programs.

Programmer
Utilized Autocoder, IBM Assembler and COBOL for program production.

EDUCATION:

DeVries University, Golden, CO   1971
Bachelor of General Studies Degree: Computer Science

EDWARD HEMINGWAY

COMBINATION

2N76 Brigantine Lane
Lowden, NE 30143
655/555-9052

PROFILE:

♦ Comprehensive technical writing skills developed through detailed product research and system documentation, including full responsibility for user manuals and reports.

♦ Interface with engineers and designers for prompt updating of all written materials, including instructional, operational and service manuals.

♦ Experience in civilian and military projects; develop specifications and oversee test reporting and variance analyses.

♦ Skilled in WordStar, PageMaker, Harvard Graphics and Ventura Publisher.

EMPLOYMENT:

<u>Motorola, Inc.</u>, Blue Glen, NE   1990-6/95
Senior Technical Writer
Performed product research and technical/nontechnical writing of operating manuals and documentation, primarily for TVs, VCRs and camcorders.
Handled writing, data compilation, layout and design of materials using desktop publishing software listed above.
Worked extensively with product designers and engineers, as well as staff in purchasing and marketing departments.
Provided full technical support and liaison functions with Sony distributors and service technicians.
Consistently transformed incomplete or confusing technical/instructional material into accurate, usable information for end users.

* Developed and utilized a modular technique that permitted consolidation of two or more similar manuals to one, resulting in a major savings in translating, printing and handling costs.
* Researched and wrote copy for 75% of all TV manuals within strict time constraints.
* Worked directly with all levels of staff and management.

<u>Kane Corporation,</u> St. Charles, NE   1986-1990
Technical Writer
Responsible for in-depth research and the writing of installation and operating manuals, service manuals and specification sheets for communication systems.
Prepared custom drawings and layouts with computer systems listed above.
Worked directly with design engineers in all departments.

* Conducted research of materials for all advanced product lines.
* Reduced technical writing staff by 19% through implementation of an on-line desktop publishing system.
* Speeded turnaround time for new product documentation by 18%.

Edward Hemingway   **Page Two**

Micrometer Engineering, Naperville, NE   1979-1986
Project Control Coordinator
Directed an entire project control task force for job scheduling, cost control and
material/document management.

* Monitored and improved the progress of engineering, procurement and
  construction activities related to the construction of power plants.
* Reorganized the document control system and developed a new methods/control
  manual; reduced labor costs 30% and labor hours from 18,000 to 10,000 per
  project.

Spielberg Petroleum Products, LaSalle, NE   1977-1979
Engineering Services Supervisor
Developed specifications and handled bidder/vendor relations and expediting in a
professional manner.
Recorded project documentation and prepared/analyzed cost reports.
Documented and analyzed variances against control budgets.

* Established and implemented engineering administrative procedures.

Eastern Corporation, Rolling Meadows, NE   1973-1979
Engineer
Primarily responsible for component evaluation and the preparation of specifications
and cost estimates.
Assisted in equipment analysis and selection.
Prepared test reports and verified compliance of materials, design and workmanship
to specifications.

* Verified — and reported on — the ability of test items to perform satisfactorily in
  various adverse environmental conditions.
* Involved in producing Electronic Countermeasure Sets used in F-15 aircraft.

General Electric Corporation, Rolling Meadows, NE   1969-1973
Equipment Engineer
Prepared and issued specifications, engineering standards and installation
procedures.
Processed/wrote software data for operating companies and provided computer
services to telephone companies in four states.

* Implemented hardware and software applications for communication systems.

EDUCATION: Cherio Graduate School, Chicago, IL   1982-1985
                     Attended courses toward M.B.A.

                     Des Plaines College, Des Plaines, IL   1977
                     B.S. Degree: Business Administration

MARVIN BUNGIE

COMBINATION

221 Ontario Lane
Streamwood, AL 47373

228/555-7385

OBJECTIVE:

MANUFACTURING / ENGINEERING
A position where solid technical skills would be utilized in thermoplastic tooling, design or injection molding.

PROFILE:

- Proven abilities in plastic injection troubleshooting, insert/two color molding, production set-ups, tool samples and capability studies.
- Skilled in CNC machinery programming, microscopes, CMMs, CIMCAD, CADKEY and Design View; proficient in Excel, Lotus 1-2-3, WordPerfect, DOS, UNIX and Macintosh systems.
- Perform tool studies; trained in metallurgy, steel tooling, jigs/fixtures, production and project management.
- Train material handlers and technicians in cost-effective procedures.

EMPLOYMENT:

Arabesque Molding, South Elgin, AL   1/93-Present
Process / Quality Engineer
Supervise/inspect production of medical and commercial injection molded plastic products on 70- to 480-ton presses.
Directly involved in production setups, tooling changes, robotics, production troubleshooting, SPC and Quality Control.
Supervise and train up to 12 employees in production and quality control procedures.
* Develop capability studies for sample injection molds.
* Perform quality audits on finished goods.
* Conduct meetings on quality control and individual worker performance.
* Write procedures for production equipment and processes.
* Maintain and document SPC of medical plastic products.

EDUCATION:

Ohio University, Athens, OH   Graduated 11/92
B.S. Degree: Industrial Technology
Minor: Business Administration   GPA: 3.1/4.0
* Four-Year Member: Society of Manufacturing Engineers.
* Self-funded 90% of college costs.
* Active in Weight Lifting Club and Habitat for Humanity.

INTERNSHIP:

APEX / Division of Cooper Industries, Dayton, OH   1990-1991
Cooperative Education Student
Interfaced with metallurgists and machinists in quality control, inspection and total product design.
Conducted surveys using salt bath heat treatment furnaces.
* Produced technical documentation from test data and maintained part gauging calibration for military aircraft universal joints.
* Performed capability studies for manufacturing engineering.
* Developed cost-saving tooling improvement methods via state-of-the-art design changes and titanium nitride coatings.

RICHARD M. CHILDS   *COMBINATION/Short Summary*
22100 Comma Road
Punctuation Hills, LA 60070
845/555-0166

OBJECTIVE: SOUS CHEF / HEAD CHEF

Profile of Experience:

- More than 12 years of professional experience in cooking and the restaurant industry, with a thorough working knowledge of regional American cuisine.
- Effectively train, supervise and motivate staff in kitchen operations.
- Creative strengths in Southwest, Caribbean and French cuisine.

Career Background:

HEAD CHEF   1987-Present
Prospector's Kitchen (American/Regional), Prospect Heights, LA
Responsible for all kitchen operations including menu planning, daily specials, ordering and food costing.
Created a seasonal menu to incorporate local ingredients in imaginative preparations.
- Prospector's Kitchen is a consistent leader in its regional market and has received critical acclaim from electronic and print media in Prospect Heights.

EXECUTIVE CHEF   1986-1987
Columbus' Hideaway (Caribbean, American/Regional), Virgin Gorda, British Virgin Islands
Supervised menu planning, daily specials, ordering and food costing.
Positioned restaurant as a successful culinary leader in the Virgin Islands.
- Created restaurant-brewed beers that sold successfully and increased bar revenue 25 percent.
- Gained experience in handling a seasonal, tourist-impacted industry.

SOUS CHEF   1984-1986
Foodtypes (Eclectic, American/Regional), Glencoe, LA
Planned menus and created daily specials.
Responsible for sautés, grilling, soups and sauces.
Handled cost-effective purchasing of all foods and equipment.
- Gained an extensive education in the use of ethnic and regional American foodstuffs.

INDEPENDENT CONTRACTOR   1978-Present
Developed ``Oasis," an independently owned and operated catering service featuring a wide variety of home-brewed beers.

ADVERTISING AND PUBLIC RELATIONS MANAGER   1978-1984
Employed as Copywriter in the advertising industry.
Subsequently became Advertising Manager for Champion Auto Parts, Inc.
Developed communication, PR and business skills that have proven invaluable in the restaurant industry.

Education:

B.S. Degree, Advertising/Journalism, Arizona State University, Tempe, AZ
American Restaurant Association   Certified for completing the Restaurant Management Program.

FERRIS A. WHEEL

COMBINATION

412 Horn View Trail
Carol Place, AZ 30188

708/555-6886

OBJECTIVE: *Engineering / Operations:* A position where hands-on skills and a strong mechanical aptitude would be utilized to benefit a growing company.

EXPERIENCE:

■ Proven abilities in virtually all aspects of engineering and plant operations, including direct responsibility for product design, processes and new startups.

■ Extensive hands-on experience with various production lines for molding, extrusion and electronic/machine assembly.

■ Analyze and streamline schedules and systems for purchasing, line assembly, upgrades and tooling to meet specific customer needs.

■ Hire, train and supervise factory workers in a strong team atmosphere; organize factory operations for low costs and high product quality.

EMPLOYMENT:

<u>NTD American</u>, Bensenville, IL   10/88-12/94
Engineer / Plant Manager
Responsible for training and supervising up to seven employees in production operations, including product assembly and quality control.
Organized shop procedures for the manufacture of pumps, heating systems/ devices and chemical dispensers for use in foam applications.
Assisted in researching and purchasing capital equipment; worked closely with vendors and suppliers.
Coordinated senior management and line workers in various operations.
Handled extensive R&D work; personally involved in retooling, parts fabrication and production streamlining for faster turnaround.
Communicate with customers to resolve problems and improve response time, while maintaining product quality to strict specifications.

* Supervised production line setups, changeovers and incoming materials.
* Analyzed problems with the established product line and designed a more efficient, stainless steel pump, which increased sales and customer satisfaction.
* Effectively reviewed, modified and upgraded temperature controllers and related systems.

<u>Basic Grigsby</u>, Chicago, IL   3/87-10/88
Manufacturing Engineer
Developed and installed new production toolings and techniques, with management responsibility for molding operations.
Repaired, fabricated and maintained mold tooling and setups.

* Solved a wide range of problems and situations on the factory floor through better communications and a no-nonsense approach to troubleshooting.

Nowtek, Inc., Chicago, IL   1/84-3/87
Contract Engineering
Produced and installed systems that used laser micrometers and microprocessors to increase line speed of plastic extruders from 1,500 ft./min to 4,000 ft./min.
Designed and produced a thermoforming machine using multilayered plastic to form 7-inch-deep food containers.
* Installed a multilayered, blown film line and a preparatory system for curing the coextruded plastic.

Belden Wire & Cable, Inc., Chicago, IL   7/80-1/84
Manufacturing and Tooling Engineer
Supervised engineering operations at five locations, including plant engineering and the design, building and troubleshooting of plastic mold tooling operations.
Personally developed new manufacturing processes and installations on the shop floor.
Directed capital budgeting and cost reduction programs.
* Directed the start-up of a completely new plant.
* Developed 25 new molds per year.
* Administered a capital budget of $1.2 million annually.
* Implemented cost-reduction programs for a savings of $400,000 annually.

Motorola, Inc., Schaumburg, IL   10/78-6/80
Manager of Planning and Facilities Construction
Managed the design, scheduling and construction of a 210,000 s.f. manufacturing, warehouse and office building valued at $4.6 million.
Administered budgets and completed this building on time and under budget.

Bensenville Home Society, Bensenville, IL   6/76-10/78
Director of Engineering
Effectively supervised staff and operations related to maintenance, purchasing, sales and procedures for new home construction.

Clow Corporation, Chicago, IL   5/70-5/76
Plant Project Engineer
Involved in energy management, equipment design and the maintenance of heat-treating ovens.
* Implemented a pollution control program.

Self-Employed: Engineering Consultant, Bloomingdale, IL   5/65-4/70

EDUCATION: University of Tennessee, Nashville, TN
                        Successful completion of numerous M.E. courses.

	COKIE V. CHUNG	*COMBINATION*
931 Prairie Drive		
Waukegan, WI 20173		708/555-6541

OBJECTIVE: *T.V. PRODUCTION / BROADCASTING*
A position where creative communication and technical skills would be utilized.

PROFILE:

- Comprehensive experience in program production including interviewing, videotaping, mixing, editing and final presentation.

- Background in weather & traffic reporting; coordinate talent and create introductions, sound bites, PSAs and professional formats.

- Hands-on experience as traffic/news reporter and talk show host for numerous programs; skilled in operating cameras and editors.

EXPERIENCE:

<u>Warner of Illinois, Inc.</u>, Mt. Prospect, IL   1993-Present
Public Access TV Producer / Playback Operator
Responsible for all aspects of development for local programs, including story origination, writing, interviews, camera operation, floor direction, sound setup and final editing.
Operate a wide range of cameras, sound boards and editors.
Manage programs from concept to completion; subjects include local artists, authors and community services.

→ Test marketed TCI's Intelligent Television project for audience control of pay-per-view movies and commercial programs.
→ Completed numerous TCI training programs in broadcasting and production.

<u>Eugenie Apartments</u>, Schaumburg, IL   Part-Time, 1989-Present
Marketing Director / Leasing Consultant
Manage all aspects of leasing for 619 residential units, including marketing, promotions and sales presentations.
Handle public relations and written/oral communications in a professional manner.
Coordinate special events and create advertisements
Assist in training and supervising three employees in creative sales, resident retention/renewal and special promotions.

→ Earned National Award for Top Sales and Customer Support.

<u>Draper & Kramer, Inc.</u>, Chicago, IL   1987-1989
Leasing Consultant

EDUCATION:

B.A. Degree: Mass Communications   Graduated 1987
<u>Rust College,</u> Holly Springs, MS

→ Employed as **Announcer / DJ** on a local radio station.
→ Earned various awards for producing and hosting a variety of talk show programs and weather, traffic and news reports.

RALPH TRACKS   *COMBINATION*

73 Nautilus Lane
Hanover, PA 40103   453/555-6393

OBJECTIVE:	A position utilizing skills developed in the railroad and shipping industries.

EXPERIENCE:

- Comprehensive background in delivery administration, merchandise inspection, returns and dispatching.

- Skilled in customer service, order tracking and billing; interact with customers and resolve problems with tact and professionalism.

- Effectively recruit, train and supervise employees; coordinate work loads and schedules.

EMPLOYMENT:

The Home Delivery Service, Arbor, PA   4/90-Present
Inspector   6/90-Present
Responsible for the check-in of delivery trucks and inspection of returned merchandise and trade-in items.
Utilize automated computer systems for manifest preparation and record keeping.
Field incoming calls from customers and resolve delivery issues.
Make calls to customers to verify deliveries and payment arrangements.
Coordinate driver schedules, cancellations and route changes.

Bay Checker   4/90-6/90
Duties included organizing/loading the dock area to meet delivery requirements.
Confirmed the accuracy of merchandise orders and maintained delivery records.
Inspected appliances, furniture and other merchandise items to verify condition.

St. Paul & Pacific/Soo Line Railroad, Bensenville, PA   6/71-11/89
Intermodal Clerk / Yard Clerk   1/79-11/89
Processed shipping orders and coordinated train departures.
Prepared/distributed bills and maintained accurate records.
Handled filing of waybills and switch lists.

Reconsigning / Weigh Clerk   9/78-1/79
Duties included reconsigning cars for industries and their brokers.
Handled rate shipping charges on bi- and tri-level cars.
Prepared bills of lading and weigh certificates; recorded carload weights and checked for overloads.

Yard Clerk / Industry Clerk   6/71-9/78
Provided customer assistance and maintained clerical records.
Handled billing and compiled information on empty car availability, route schedules, releases, car transfers and switches.

EDUCATION: East Layden High School, Franklin Park, PA   Graduate

STEVEN J. NAYOB

COMBINATION

110 Mural Lane
Mt. Prospect, IL 60056

708/555-0211

OBJECTIVE:

LOAN OFFICER
A position where proven analytical skills would be utilized.

PROFILE:

- More than three years in cost analyses, credit and securities operations, with full responsibility for account tracking and updating.

- Experience in construction loan administration; familiar with related credit approval forms and procedures.

- Compile and present spreadsheets and reports; skilled in Lotus, Harvard Graphics, WordPerfect, Paradox, PC tools and various database management systems.

- Assist in marketing, portfolio management and risk analysis; perform wire transfers and general administration with legal, credit and collateral personnel; provide full customer service and support.

- Skilled in general accounting, collections, problem resolution and the writing of customer correspondence.

EMPLOYMENT:

First Chicago Bank, Chicago, IL
1988-Present

Marketing Assistant / Second Assistant Loan Officer
1990-Present
Work directly with loan officers and provide support in credit and administration for major construction loans.
Manage a network of 20 PCs and design/utilize cash flow models on R.E.P.A., a computerized real estate project analysis system.
Train personnel in computer system use on a continual basis.

* Communicate with staff and assist in cash management, as well as the administration of letters of credit.
* Interface with lenders and loan personnel in a professional, yet personalized manner.

Analyst
1988-1990
Responsible for order expediting and the constant review/management of risks and cash flows.
Tracked outstanding accounts and the timeliness of funding for specific projects.
Performed data input, wire transfers and various credit-related functions.

* Completed bank training in internal credit procedures.

<u>Loftus and Omera,</u> Chicago, IL   1987-1988
Accounting Assistant
Transferred and verified accounting records on a computerized system for a major chemical testing firm.

<u>Superior Temporary,</u> Elk Grove Village, IL   Summers, 1986-1987
Warehouseman
Processed orders and worked with management in a prompt, professional manner.

<u>Jeffrey Laundromat,</u> Carbondale, IL   2/86-5/86
Manager
Accepted all profit/loss responsibilities for sales, accounting and procedures at this coin-operated laundromat.

EDUCATION: <u>Southern Illinois University,</u> Carbondale, IL   1991
B.S. Degree -- Finance and Business

* Completed a major project involving an in-depth case study simulating a business. Planned and implemented effective financial controls and improved levels of productivity.
* Raised status of the company to 18th from 57th.

Activities:

* Floor Representative, 1983
* Student Life Advisor - Student Orientation, 1983
* Vice President, Hall Council, 1984
* Social Chairman, Intervarsity Christian Fellowship, 1985
* President, Intervarsity Christian Fellowship, 1986 and 1987.
* Member of Speaker Committee, Financial Management Association, 1988.

WILBUR NECKI   *COMBINATION*

139 Whitehall Street
Dearborn, TX 20047   328/555-8231

OBJECTIVE:	***AVIATION / LAW ENFORCEMENT*** A position utilizing experience in criminal investigations, customs and/or professional flying.

PROFILE:

- Assist in investigations, including searches, seizures and subject interviewing; well versed in customs regulations and procedures.

- Licensed private pilot, with 210 Hours and Instrument Rating; experience with various Beechcraft and Cessna planes.

- Accredited Military Customs Agent; handle confiscations and apprehensions of violent and nonviolent subjects.

MILITARY:

<u>U.S. Air Force,</u> Nurnberg, Germany   11/84-11/87
Investigator / Military Policeman   7/86-11/87
Investigated black market trading between soldiers and German civilians.
Handled surveillance and tracking of subjects.
* As Accredited U.S. Military Customs Agent, conducted searches and cleared aircraft in Europe bound for the U.S.
* Apprehended, arrested and interviewed perpetrators and seized all types of goods: tobacco, alcohol, clothing, electronics and various weapons.

CIVILIAN EMPLOYMENT:

<u>Streamwood YMCA,</u> Streamwood, IL   Part Time 12/93-Present
Building Supervisor
Manage building facilities, security and personnel.

<u>Wilson Hospital Supply Co.,</u> Lake Zurich, TX   Part Time 7/88-7/93
Receiving / Warehouseman
Responsible for prompt receiving and storage of hospital supplies.
Updated and maintained inventory reports on a daily basis.

<u>Venus Club,</u> San Antonio, TX   Pt. Time 8/88-8/89
Doorman
Maintained safe and secure operations at this large capacity night club; managed drunk/disorderly patrons in a professional manner.

<u>Guardsman Security Services,</u> Libertyville, TX   1/88-8/88
Security Guard

EDUCATION:

<u>Lewis University,</u> Romeoville, TX
B.S. Degree: Aviation Administration   Graduated 5/92
Overall GPA: 3.3/4.0 Major GPA: 3.5/4.0
* Completed flight training through the Aviation Administration.

CLAUDIUS PORT   *COMBINATION*

1225 North Wood Street
Tacoma, WA 30067   128/555-7895

PRODUCT DEVELOPMENT / TECHNICAL SUPPORT

EXPERIENCE:

- Comprehensive skills in component and system-level repair and testing of electronic equipment; work directly with engineers and production staff at virtually all levels of experience.

- Assist in sales presentations and negotiate contracts; determine and meet client's specific product needs in a professional manner.

- Handle procedure planning and implementation, as well as job scheduling and business system streamlining.

- Background in promotions and general marketing; proven ability to develop referral business through personalized customer service.

EMPLOYMENT:

Thiokol, Inc., Tacoma, WA   1979-4/94
Senior Electronic Technician   1984-4/94
Involved in the development and sale of radar and advanced avionics equipment to the U.S. government.
Documented product specifications and functions through research and technical writing of reports; analyzed and corrected design flaws in a variety of systems for advanced bomber and fighter aircraft.
* Responsible for efficient production scheduling through interface with senior-level management and engineers.
* Conducted in-depth contract and blueprint interpretation for the clientele.
* Analyzed and streamlined all related production and sales procedures.
* Trained numerous workers in the use of testing and production equipment.

Electronic Technician   1982-1984
Maintained excellent product quality through testing with class ``B'' equipment, including oscilloscopes and spectrum & spectral analyzers.

Repair Technician   1980-1982
Solderer / Assembler   1979-1980

Mrs. Rosenthal's Place Tacoma, WA   2/91-Present
Owner / Operator
Perform all sales and marketing at this painting and remodeling service.
Quote prices and negotiate sales contracts; design/place creative advertising and promotions.
Train and supervise personnel in effective customer service and job procedures.

EDUCATION:

William Forest College, Tacoma, WA   1985
Completed more than 40 credit hours in Electronics and Mathematics.

ROGER ARCHAMBALDT, CIC, ARM

CHRONOLOGICAL with Conservative Summary

151 Falls Street
Laramie, WY 30123

558/555-8765

RISK MANAGEMENT AND UNDERWRITING PROFESSIONAL

Executive-level skills in risk management, innovative problem solving and operations management.
Thirteen years of diversified insurance experience includes management, underwriting and claims handling.

EXPERIENCE

Chico National Insurance Company (A subsidiary of Peterbilt International Transportation Corp.)
Laramie, WY   1989-Present
Vice President, Underwriting and Administration

Determine and manage underwriting guidelines, loss control, policy rating and processing for all lines of business in 48 states. Directly responsible for supervising 52 employees and administering a $2.8 million department budget. Diverse coverages include property, garage and auto liability, workers' compensation and umbrella.

- Developed and implemented underwriting manuals and procedures for Long Haul Trucking, Auto Lease/Rental and General Agent Guidelines.
- Reduced loss ratio by 3.1 percent during Fiscal Year 1990 and 4.9 percent during FY 1991.
- $100,000 under budget in 1991, during a significant $3.9 million increase in written premiums.
- Initiated and structured an in-house Loss Control Department.
- Highly skilled at motivating and focusing activities of diverse departments to accomplish goals.
- Active Member of the N.A.I.I. Trucker's Committee since 1989.

National Farmers Union Insurance Companies - Denver, CO   1983-1989
Commercial Underwriting Manager   1989
Senior Account Manager - Corporate Accounts   1985-1989
Account Manager (Underwriter)   1983-1985

Directly responsible for all aspects of risk selection and underwriting for Farm Cooperatives and Telephone Companies with premiums ranging from $50,000 to $1 million.
Coverages included directors' and officers' property, general and auto liability, workers' compensation and umbrella.

- Cowrote the company package policy for Special Accounts.
- Developed and implemented a procedure manual for General Agents and Commercial Underwriters.

Roger Archambaldt, CIC, ARM   **Page Two**

_____

<u>Progressive Casualty Insurance Company</u> - Denver, CO   1979-1983
Senior Claims Adjuster

Controlled each claim from inception to settlement for both high-risk auto, motorcycle and property lines. Negotiated settlements with claimants and/or representing attorneys.

- Assessed and established loss reserves.
- Successfully covered a multistate territory.

<u>Proctor and Gamble Distribution Company</u> - Englewood, CO   1978-1979
Institutional Sales Representative

Involved in the sale and marketing of Commercial/Institutional Cleaning and Soap products in Colorado and Wyoming.

- Facilitated the introduction of Comet Liquid.

<u>Green River High School</u> - Green River, WY   1976-1978
Teacher / Coordinator of Distributive Education (Marketing)

Responsible for teaching three marketing courses and coordinating 45 students in off-site, part-time employment.

- Promoted to Department Head of Program in 1977.
- Sponsor of DECA Club (extracurricular).
- Member of the School District Curriculum Committee.

EDUCATION

<u>University of Wyoming,</u> Laramie, WY
Completed several courses toward a Master's Degree in Business Administration.

<u>Colorado State University (CSU),</u> Ft. Collins, CO
B.E. Degree, Education   Graduated 1976
- Graduated First in Class with Highest Distinction.

CERTIFICATIONS / AWARDS

Associate in Risk Management (ARM)   1988
- Award for Academic Excellence at CPCU Awards Ceremony.

Certified Insurance Counselor (CIC)   1985

<u>American Educational Institute</u>   1983
Certified for completion of a course in Legal Principles.

MILES DISTANCE

COMBINATION

2244 Apple Avenue
Deerfield, KS 11315

445/555-9246

OBJECTIVE:

RESTAURANT MANAGEMENT
A position where solid leadership skills would be utilized.

PROFILE:

- Experience in the setup and management of restaurant and hotel operations, including full P&L responsibilities.

- Coordinate payroll, AP/AR and general ledger maintenance, as well as inventory control; implement labor and cost controls; create daily sales and P&L reports on various computer systems.

- Sanitation Certified; conduct on-the-job training and supervision of front and back-house staff in food preparation, sanitation and effective customer service.

- Plan and implement menus for banquets and special events; coordinate co-op and in-house advertising, as well as sales promotions.

- Manage all aspects of budgeting, forecasting, purchasing and marketing; track sales of individual food and beverage items on a daily basis.

EMPLOYMENT:

Miller's Backhouse, Deerfield, MA

1990-Present

Manager
Effectively train and supervise more than 70 employees in all front & back house operations for this major downtown restaurant.
Conduct group and individual training of kitchen and wait staff; formulate job classifications, develop work incentives and evaluate worker performance.

- * Update and maintain daily P&L statements and manage all general accounting functions: AP/AR, payroll and general ledgers.
- * Oversee employee benefit and insurance activities.
- * Utilize an Amdahl computer to track daily sales of individual food and beverage items.
- * Handle cost-effective purchasing of all food, beverages, equipment and supplies, with excellent vendor relations.

Blue Terrace Hotel, Wauconda, MA

1988-1990

Owner / General Manager
Responsible for all sales, marketing and more than 20 employees at this full-service restaurant with a capacity of 275.
Supervised all customer service activities, as well as purchasing and inventory control.

- * Created and marketed banquet plans for a variety of businesses and community organizations.

Jerry's Pine Log Restaurant, Skokie, MA   1972-1988
General Manager / Owner
Directed hiring, training and scheduling functions for more than 70 employees, including introduction of a three-step, on-the-job training program with seminars and video instruction. Conducted monthly meetings for employee feedback and brainstorming to improve operations and morale.
Formalized job classifications and evaluated worker performance.
Worked directly with bookkeeping staff to track and process all data related to payroll, AP/AR, cost controls, food and liquor.

* Responsible for all marketing, promotions and advertising.
* Designed employee recognition programs and increased the sale of wine, dessert and after-drink purchases.
* Increased sales through co-op advertising programs with American Express Corporation, local beer/wine purveyors and food vendors.
* Improved banquet sales and promotions with package plans for numerous organizations, including civic groups and large businesses: Marshall Fields & Company, Gingiss Formal Wear, Seno & Sons, schools, churches and synagogues.

At this restaurant *and* at the Blue Terrace Hotel:

* Reduced payroll preparation costs 5 percent by using outside data processing services.
* Lowered payroll 3 percent by restructuring salaried worker's status to an hourly rate scale.
* Decreased liquor costs 4 percent by restructuring purchasing procedures.
* Lowered discount rates charged by major credit card companies by 50 percent.
* Reduced liability insurance premiums by 10 percent.
* Consolidated total insurance premiums with one common carrier.

CERTIFICATION: State of Massachusetts Sanitation Certified.

EDUCATION: Loyola University of Chicago, Chicago, IL
B.A. Degree: Business Administration   1972

SkyView College, Dubuque, IA   1971
Completed courses in Business Administration.

LINDA B. WINKLER   *COMBINATION: Career Change*

4379 North Southport
Chicago, IL 60608   448/555-0275

REAL ESTATE APPRAISER

PROFILE:
- Trained in *[or Experience in]* full property assessment including measuring, picture taking, evaluation of comparative properties and the preparation of final reports.

- Completed studies in Real Estate Appraisal Principles at The Appraisal Institute in Chicago; currently working toward SRA designation.

EMPLOYMENT:
Eichmann & Associates, Westchester, CT
Research Assistant   1991-Present
Maintain thousands of files and a computer-based employee tracking system for the M.I.S./Mainframe Division.
Independently research accounts and provide administrative support to data entry staff.

Grover Place Restaurant, Bloomingdale, IL
Waiter   1990-1991
Coordinated side-station duties, assisted in problem solving and served as host.

Barnum Clothiers, Bloomington, IL
Sales Associate   1989-1989
Employed aggressive sales techniques to consistently achieve or exceed weekly goals.
Handled nightly department closings and provided direct customer service.

White Hen Pantry, Hinsdale, IL
Assistant Manager   1985-1986
Trained, scheduled and supervised up to 10 employees.
Responsible for inventory control, purchasing and cash management.

EDUCATION:
Illinois State University, Normal, IL
Bachelor of Science Degree: Political Science   Graduated 1990
Minor in Criminal Justice Sciences

- Delta Chi Fraternity: GAMMA Committee Representative and PR Committee, Fall 1988 to Fall 1990
- Illinois State University Law Club, Fall 1988 to Spring 1989
- Illinois State University Tae Kwon Do Club, Fall 1985 to Spring 1987

With the Risk Management Committee under GAMMA:
- Implemented and organized the Greek Designated Driver Program in conjunction with local drinking establishments.
- Developed and designed pamphlets to provide necessary information and promote responsibility in planning social gatherings.

JOHN MELLON

COMBINATION

331 Phillippi Drive
Hot Springs, AK 50120

432/555-1199

OBJECTIVE:	**Management: International Freight Forwarding** A position where profit-building skills would be utilized.

PROFILE:

♦ Proven management skills in virtually all import/export operations, including full profit/loss responsibilities.

♦ Experience in recruiting, training and supervising staff and management in customs regulations, freight forwarding, routing, sales and marketing.

♦ Budget planning and sales forecasting; skilled in financial statement preparation and analysis; familiar with Lotus 1-2-3.

♦ Experience in full warehouse and multisite supervision; fluent in Spanish.

EMPLOYMENT: Tony Corporation, Hot Springs, AK   3/89-3/94

Regional Vice President
Responsible for six midwest offices and more than 60 employees at the Chicago location.
Directed six managers and their staff, a total of 117 employees.
Created and administered all budgets for the Chicago office and analyzed/approved budgets for all six offices.
Directed domestic and international air freight as well as customs brokerage.
Coordinated ocean import/export, container services and inbound/outbound ocean freight.
In charge of overall sales and productivity, including staff training and motivation.

* Consistently determined and met sales targets.
* Managed all operations at a 32,000 s.f. warehouse.
* Gross 1991 profit exceeded $4 million in the Chicago office alone.
* Reduced staff while increasing productivity and speed of order processing.
* Planned, implemented and improved all sales and marketing strategies with an extensive knowledge of competitors, air/sea carriers and the clientele.

Rainey Robinson Company, Bensenville, AK   1970-3/89

Vice President / Regional Manager   1984-3/89
Directed sales, marketing and all shipping & import/export operations for this firm specializing in customs brokerage, ocean shipping and sales.
Managed over 60 staff and managers at locations in Cleveland, Detroit, Chicago, Minneapolis and St. Louis.

* Three-time Employee of the Month, 1988.

Midwest Regional Manager 1975-1984

Effectively hired, trained and supervised up to 25 employees in import/export operations and customer service.

* Personally set up and opened the highly successful St. Louis and Detroit offices.

Branch Manager 1970-1975

In charge of the Chicago branch office with more than 35 support personnel and three supervisors.

Nettles & Company, Bensenville, AK 1967-1970

Manager / Corporate Secretary

Responsible for all export operations and air/ocean freight.
Directly involved in the setup of this entire company, including office procedure planning, market penetration and sales.

* Assisted in budget preparation, sales forecasting and financial planning.

EDUCATION: Northwestern Illinois University, Evanston, AK

Successful completion of two seminars in Transportation, including training in railroad and import/export operations.

Xerox Corporation
Completed training in professional selling skills.

Dale Carnegie Management Course
Completed extensive Management training programs.

High School Graduate

INTERESTS: Enjoy Golf, Boating, Music and all Sports.

THOMAS SENDER   *COMBINATION*

1987 Burroughs Drive
Vicksburg, PA 30108   877/255-2563

OBJECTIVE: A position utilizing experience in vendor relations and the cost-effective management of purchasing functions.

PROFILE:
- More than 14 years in virtually all aspects of purchasing, including full responsibility for department setup, procedures and management.

- Skilled in vendor/material sourcing and price negotiation; organize buyers and suppliers in major international markets.

- Experience in new product development, cost reduction and inventory control; proficient in MRP II and JIT system implementation and user training.

- Plan and conduct vendor quality audits; organize component purchasing and subcontracting procedures.

- Effectively hire, train and supervise buyers and support staff at virtually all levels of experience.

EMPLOYMENT: <u>Lightening Bolt, Inc.</u>, Vicksburg, PA   1985-Present
Purchasing Manager
In charge of all aspects of a multimillion dollar purchasing department for a major manufacturer of equipment for the fast food industry.
Coordinate buyers and support staff in the sourcing and purchase of raw materials, electronic components, plastics, machine parts and sheet metal goods.
Interface with engineers and department managers; supervise purchasing functions related to new product development, contract negotiations and subcontracting for machining operations.
Aggressively research and secure competitive prices on all required parts and components, resulting in substantial cost savings.
Perform quality audits of suppliers; provide corrective action and follow-up audits.

* Installed computerized MRP II systems within the purchasing department.
* Researched and implemented software systems to evaluate purchased product cost, availability, on-time delivery and quality on both a department and company-wide basis.
* Effectively cross-trained personnel to ensure adequate coverage of all commodities.
* Created, implemented and improved bills of material.
* Established a cost reduction program with several suppliers; lowered costs while improving both quality and speed of delivery.
* Sourced new products and greatly reduced preliminary costs.

<u>Radical Systems, Inc.,</u> Itasca, PA   1981-1985
Purchasing Agent
Established an entire purchasing department from the zero for this multimillion dollar producer of air and hydraulic cylinder accessories.
Developed manuals and planned/implemented all policies and procedures.
* Purchased castings and forgings; maintained excellent part quality.
* Aggressively sourced component parts & supplies.
* Reported directly to the company president.

<u>Weiser Fluid Power Inc.,</u> Superville, PA   1966-1981
Various Purchasing positions, most recent first:

Purchasing Department Supervisor
Managed a purchasing department of 14 for this firm which manufactured and distributed air and hydraulic cylinders and related equipment.
* Reduced inventory by 10 percent; ensured a continuous availability of parts.
* Updated machining practices and reduced rejected, subcontracted parts by 25 percent; lowered related costs by 10 percent.
* Converted production of various parts from casting to forging; reduced rejection rate and machining costs by 10 percent; lowered lead time by 50 percent.

Senior Buyer
Trained and evaluated new buyers and assisted in a steady transition to a more complex product line.
* Worked directly with engineers in part design and tolerance updating; saved 30 percent annually and reduced costs in custom part production while speeding delivery time.
* Assisted engineers in material upgrades, resulting in annual savings of 25 percent on piece parts and 10 percent on rejects damaged in assembly.
* Developed a new product line introduced six months prior to the competition; substantially increasing gross sales.

Buyer
Recommended alternatives and upgrades for steel and plastic materials, monitored costs, sourced vendors and created competitive pricing.

Order Writer

EDUCATION: <u>Ellyn Community College,</u> Red Ellyn, PA
                  A.A.S. Degree   1979

                  <u>Wilbur Wright MRP II Classes</u>   Six Months, 1992

SYLVIA D. CAPER   *COMBINATION*

2214 Newton Street
Wallaby, MA 30084   548/555-9521

OBJECTIVE: A position in the Radiology department of a major hospital or clinic, where proven supervisory skills would be of value.

EXPERIENCE:
- Comprehensive skills in MRI department activities, including responsibility for patient relations and staff hiring, training and supervision.

- Developed and conducted an MRI certification program at Triton College, 8/89; Coauthor of an article on MRI equipment which appeared in *Radiology* magazine.

- Schedule and organize all MRI procedures; skilled in the use of G.E. 1.5 and .5 Tesla Technicare scanners for brain, cervical, thoracic, abdomen, lumbar spine and extremity analysis.

EMPLOYMENT: The Winter's Radiology Institute, Crystal Lake, MA   7/85-Present
Chief Technologist - Magnetic Resonance Imaging Department
Manage virtually all MRI department activities and the training, supervision and coordination of up to 12 technologists and darkroom staff.
Schedule/expedite patients care and work directly with physicians; review patient's clinical history for scanning and photography.
Oversee all documentation and filing procedures, as well as examinations listed above for inpatients and outpatients.
Operate remote and operator consoles, as well as terminal equipment; select and modify technical factors as required.
Prepare room equipment, medications and infusion materials.
Question patients and thoroughly explain all procedures.

* Reduced MRI staff turnover by 30 percent.
* Increased MRI patient throughput by 12 percent each year since 1985.

EDUCATION: Sherwood Forest College, Lake Forest, IL   1981-1983
Successful completion of courses in Biochemistry.

SEMINARS &
TRAINING: The Medical College of Alaska, Fairbanks, AL   4/90
Courses included FastScan MRI and clinical applications of gradient echos.
Attended a pathology demonstration of spin echo/gradient echo crossovers.

Anthony Joseph Business Programs   6/91
Completed an eight-week course in Effective Time Management.

PUBLICATION: *Radiology Magazine* - 211 (p) 72
Cowrote ``H-1 MR Spectroscopy of Human Tumors In Vivo."

NIKKI ZELLO

COMBINATION

4562 Kangaroo Lane
Schaumburg, IL 60194

708/555-7063

OBJECTIVE:

FLIGHT ATTENDANT - *Willing to travel or relocate.*
A position with Delta Airlines, where proven skills would be utilized.

PROFILE:

- More than four years in customer service and professional communications, including responsibility for troubleshooting and work flow organizing.

- Speak conversational German; traveled throughout Germany, Austria, Canada, Hawaii and the continental U.S.

- Height: 5'6", 131 lbs; professional modeling experience for a major fragrance company; selected for advanced modeling courses at the Barbizon School of Modeling.

- Strong knowledge of first-aid; Red Cross Certified in Junior Lifesaving.

EMPLOYMENT:

The Purple Garden Restaurant, Bloomingdale, IL   1/91-Present
Hostess
Organize and track seating for hundreds of customers daily at this busy Italian restaurant.
Greet customers in a professional manner and provide prompt, courteous service.
* Train new employees in hosting and seating.

Carlos Murphy's, Schaumburg, IL   1/90-12/90
Hostess
Developed customer volume reports every 30 minutes.
Greeted and directed hundreds of patrons to their tables promptly and politely.
* Answer telephone calls quickly and professionally.

Schaumburg Park District, Schaumburg, IL   Winter, 1987-1988
Ice Skating Supervisor
Monitored skaters and the safety of skating conditions.
Completed accident reports and performed on-the-spot first aid as needed.

EDUCATION:

Prince Albert College, Palatine, IL
Completed a Psychology course.   1990

Barbizon School of Modeling, Chicago, IL
Graduated from Modeling courses.   1989

Hoffman High School, Hoffman Estates, IL   Graduated 1988

PERSONAL:

Skated Competitively for nine years, including six years in precision skating.
Church Usher at Church of the Holy Spirit, Schaumburg.
Enjoy skating, skiing and bicycling.

DEAN JAIN   COMBINATION

4333 Washington Street
South Bend, IN 90103   321/555-0795

OBJECTIVE:	A position in Architectural Design, utilizing training and experience in creative drafting and project management.

PROFILE:

- More than three years in design, drafting and blueprint development, including full project management responsibilities.

- Experience in job costing, price quoting and professional customer service; plan and conduct written & oral presentations for executive clientele.

- Extensive training in the design of residential/commercial buildings and steel structures, as well as plot surveying and layout.

EMPLOYMENT:

Aspiration Tools, Inc., South Bend, IN   1988-Present
Engineering Draftsman - Engineering Services
Design and draft a wide range of electrical connectors for automotive, industrial and ordnance applications.
Perform full project cost estimating and price quoting.
Effectively manage projects from concept to completion, including extensive customer relations for design updates and troubleshooting.
Compile and present written proposals, estimates and presentations.

- Provide back-up to the blueprint department, distributing blueprints and plans to various companies and plants nationwide.
- Developed configurations for office floors and efficient placement of computer workstations, tables and filing systems.

Crawford Risk Management, South Bend, IN   1987-1988
Documentation Department
Worked extensively with adjusters and organized, updated and prepared courtroom files on a computer system.

Target Credit Central, South Bend, IN   1977-1987
Customer Service Representative
Responsible for heavy telephone communications with customers regarding credit and account status.
Updated and maintained numerous files on a computer system.

EDUCATION:

University of Chicago, Chicago, IL   Graduated 8/91
B.S. Degree: Architecture   GPA: 3.5/4.0

Evanston College, Evanston, IL
Successful completion of Architectural courses, 1986-1988.
- Planned and conducted classes in Architecture, requiring student motivation and evaluation.

JOHN D. EDWARDS

CHRONOLOGICAL

922 Wakeby Lane
Shreveport, LA 40193   328/555-5474

OBJECTIVE: A position as Chief of Police, where a strong commitment to public service and more than 15 years of leadership in law enforcement would be utilized.

EXPERIENCE: <u>Sheriffs Department,</u> Baton Rouge, LA   11/91-Present
Deputy Sheriff
Spearheaded a special D.U.I. Task Force, including the screening and management of 12 officers in the detection and apprehension of impaired drivers.
Area of scope includes all waterways within Baton Rouge.
Accepted Task Force management duties in addition to those of a patrol unit.

<u>Village of Gilberts, LA</u>   7/90-11/91
Police Officer: Currently on leave of absence
In addition to regular Police Officer duties, effectively instituted and managed *Project Management for Accreditation*, which included the writing and implementation of policies and procedures.
Responsible for building interdepartmental skills and relations within the Gilberts Police Department and with the Sheriffs department.
Directed seven employees and their accreditation, involving extensive training and development.
Assisted in reviewing and purchasing computer software and hardware for the networking of records.

* Started the Z.A.P. Program to encourage youth to reject commercials that encourage drinking.
* Developed and managed the A.I.M. (Alliance Against Intoxicated Motorists) and M.A.D.D. (Mothers Against Drunk Driving) programs.
* Initiated the *Notice of Minor Violation* program, which increased the General Revenue Fund by 80 percent.
* Supervised fundraising efforts for the 1991 Gilbert's Police Department Benevolent Association. Committed to contacting local businesses to raise money for equipment. Increased revenue from the previous year from $700 to more than $4,000.
* As Field Training officer, trained new officers in department policies and procedures and taught interdepartment classes.
* Wrote a grant for the department this year to the Illinois Department of transportation for the purchase of a breathalyzer.
* Planned and implemented procedures for a Warrants Program and physically served warrants as needed.

John D. Edwards   **Page Two**

United States Department of Energy, Various Locations   1/89-7/90
Federal Officer
Responsible for the protection of life and property of federal employees at nuclear installations. Currently on leave of absence.

Venture Transportation, Inc., Shreveport, LA   3/84-8/90
President / CEO
In charge of all operations and facilities for this transportation, brokerage and forwarding service, including fiscal/executive management, sales and marketing. Recruited carriers, acquired real estate and developed/administered budgets.

* Implemented a computer system for dispatch and commodities control, as well as programs for warehousing, physical distribution, storage and consolidation.
* Worked closely with personnel in air freight, LTL/full truck shipments and rail.
* Managed sales and marketing, including brochures, radio and telecommunications; wrote sales materials and contracts for carriers.

Police Officer and Deputy Sheriff, various departments   1978-1987
Gained more than ten years of experience in all aspects of patrol and law enforcement, including patrol duty on rotating shifts and traffic enforcement.
Enforced DUI programs and assisted in detective work.
* Worked in the jail, served warrants and acted as Road Deputy.

SPECIALIZED TRAINING:

* Illinois State Police Training Academy
* Missouri Highway Patrol Training Academy
* Federal Officer's Training Academy
* Northern Illinois Truck Enforcement School
* Breathalyzer Operator - Certified IDPH
* Legal aspects of department discipline
* Financial investigation/white collar crime
* Team building
* Criminal procedure and civil liability
* Completed training for Project Management for Accreditation

EDUCATION: Oakton College, Des Plaines, IL   General Business Courses, 1991

LaSalle University, Chicago, IL   Juris Doctor Student, 1992

Northwestern University, Evanston, IL
Attended several law enforcement management seminars in April of 1991.
Topics included Department Management and Human Resources.

TERRANCE REYERSON   *COMBINATION*

987 Ramble Street
Madison, WI 30101   328/555-2951

OBJECTIVE: A position as Claims Adjuster, utilizing proven abilities in data management and communications.

PROFILE:
- Strong working knowledge of CICS/Unimatic, TSO/Focus computer systems and Lotus 1-2-3.

- Skilled in database management and operations analysis in high-pressure situations; perform audits of customer accounts, legal files and airline flight information.

- Analyze and write status reports on a full range of operations for corporate management; train assistants on contractual research procedures.

EMPLOYMENT:

Kiwi Airlines Inc., Madison, WI   12/89-Present
Data Controller   5/91-Present
Responsible for processing flight data including passenger, cargo and flight schedules. Assist the group manager in streamlining weekly operations and promptly correct improperly formatted data.

* Earned Certificate for no sick days or late attendance.
* Promoted to this position from:

Administrative Assistant   12/89-5/91
Maintained contract and document files in the corporate legal library.
Identified incomplete contracts and initiated corrective action.

Charter Bank, Madison, WI   9/89-12/89
Customer Service Representative
Responsible for general financial transactions and customer relations.
Handled customer account maintenance and data entry/retrieval; familiar with the IBM 4704 Teller System.

Locktite Corporation, Madison, WI   1985-1987
Assembler
Assembled and/or repaired bus and train doors.
Carried a full college course load while working 20 hours each week.

EDUCATION:

University of Whitewater, Whitewater, WI   1985-1989
B.S. Degree: Mathematics

* Major GPA: 4.0/5.0
* Active Member of the Filipino Club.
* Volunteer for the United Way Charitable Program, 1991.

DAVID MILKE   *COMBINATION*

3339 Hazelnut Drive   127/555-6591 Ofc.
Brooklyn, NY 10107   127/555-1839 Res.

PROFILE:

- More than 15 years of combined experience in domestic and international petrochemical and power plant construction, engineering, inspection and power plant outage work, including full department management.

- Direct experience in stressful and hostile environments at power and petrochemical plants in the Middle East.

- Skilled in virtually all phases of civil, mechanical, structural and electrical construction inspection.

- Develop and implement quality control procedures; conduct independent design verification reviews and ASME XI ISI baseline inspections of nuclear steam supply system (NSSS) piping.

- Experience as Lead Engineer; handle staff training, supervision and communications in a professional manner; interface with vendors and clients at all levels of experience.

- Assist in writing and reviewing equipment specifications, welding/NDE procedures and installation instructions; perform source surveillance inspections on nuclear and fossil plant equipment.

EMPLOYMENT:

Sergeant & Lefty Engineers, Brooklyn, NY   11/89-Present
Quality Control Engineer: Various locations/assignments:

Currently based in Brooklyn, NY - Q.C. Division   3/91-Present
Responsible for coordinating the submittal, review and acceptance of equipment vendor procedures for Point Aconi (fossil fuel) Power Station, Nova Scotia, Canada.

Tennessee Valley Authority, Watts Bar Nuclear Station
Spring City, TN   6/90-3/91
Performed electrical system and HVAC support walkdowns, including data compilation and the preparation of as-built field sketches.
Completed documentation for critical case evaluations in response to concerns generated by the NRC.

Chicago, IL   11/89-6/90
Coordinated the preparation of ASME code and material reconciliations for use at all Commonwealth Edison Nuclear Stations.
Provided full construction surveillance support at Schahfer Unit 14 during hot to cold precipitation modification.

Properties of America, Williamstown, MA   3/87-5/89
Associate Land Consultant, Senior Land Consultant and Sales Manager
Promoted to several positions in Maine, New Hampshire and Vermont.
Planned and conducted sales presentations and supervised sales staff.
Assisted in marketing and budget administration.

<u>Stone & Webster Engineering Corporation,</u> various assignments   3/74-4/86
Senior QC Engineer
Turkey Point Nuclear Power Plant, Homestead, FL   11/85-4/86
Performed radiography and film interpretation of piping systems, vessels and welders' test coupons.

Superintendent of Quality Control   12/82-10/85
Aramco Marjan Gas Oil Separation Plant, Tanajib, Saudi Arabia
In charge of inspection aspects of this project from initial construction to final client acceptance.
Effectively controlled departmental budgets.
Supervised NDT contractors and vendor surveillance personnel.
Prepared certification of concrete batch plants and vendor qualifications.

QC Engineer   1/82-11/82
Field QC Headquarters Group, Boston, MA
Wrote and revised new and existing FQC procedures and guidelines.

Welding Supervisor   9/80-12/81
Azzawiya Ethylene Complex, Ras Lanuf, Libya
Effectively monitored welding and NDT operations of contractors.
Coordinated the resolution of all technical problems through interface with the London office and resolved routine site problems in absence of Senior Welding Engineer.

Associate QC Engineer   3/74-5/80
Shoreham Nuclear Power Plant, Wading River, NY
Performed welding and NDT inspection on piping systems, supports and appurtenances.

EDUCATION: <u>Northeastern University,</u> Boston, MA
Bachelor of Science Degree: Industrial Technology, 1974

<u>Wentworth Institute,</u> Boston, MA
Associate of Applied Science Degree: Aeronautical Technology, 1973

<u>NDT Schools:</u> Additional Training through Stone & Webster Engineering.
Earned Level II NDT Certifications in Ultrasonic, Radiography and Film Interpretation.

JIMMY C. HODDING   *COMBINATION*
123 Hillside Court
Boston, MA 20103
128/555-4142

OBJECTIVE: A *Paralegal* position where communication and organizational skills would
be utilized.

EXPERIENCE: → Skilled in research, legal writing and the preparation of case studies using Westlaw and
the Lexus system.

→ Trained in real estate - currently a Licensed Agent; knowledge of probate and
corporate/securities law, as well as contracts, litigation and adjudication.

→ Handle filings with various government agencies; provide trial and hearing support in
a professional manner.

EMPLOYMENT: <u>Perez & Nordquist,</u> Newark, NJ   1982-Present
Paralegal / Messenger
Provide trial/hearing support for this law office with 32 attorneys.
Conduct legal research at the Library Of Congress, as well as detailed investigations and
legal writing.
Handle filings with the S.E.C. and the departments of Trade and Commerce.
*   Act as messenger for important, time-sensitive materials.
*   Ensure accuracy of all written and oral communications.

<u>The Podgorniak Law Firm, Inc.,</u> Washington, D.C.   1974-1982
Paralegal
Specialized in corporate and tax law, litigation and real estate matters.
Incorporated new businesses, prepared corporate minutes and summarized depositions.
Analyzed/prepared closing documents and checked facts and statements for appeals.
*   Corresponded extensively with clients regarding case status and bankruptcy petitions.
*   Drafted wills and performed detailed legal research.

<u>Buckolz Club International,</u> Evanston, IL   1972-1974
General Office Clerk
Responsible for extensive correspondence writing and distribution in support of the Director
of Communications.
Handled data entry, record keeping and the preparation of custom documents.

EDUCATION: <u>American Institute for Paralegal Studies, Inc.,</u> Oakbrook Terrace, IL
Certified Paralegal   Graduated 7/74

GARY S. KISIAN   *COMBINATION*

9898 Baltic Drive
Nashville, TN 43194   328/555-6155

EXPERIENCE:
- More than five years in staff training and supervision, including full responsibility for training programs and leadership.

- Successful in teaching professional customer service and communications methods to groups and individuals.

- Familiar with PageMaker, Excel and Windows for the writing of training manuals and customer correspondence; familiar with various Macintosh software.

EMPLOYMENT:
Zenith Training Systems, Nashville, TN   11/85-Present
Customer Service Trainer / Consultant   11/89-Present
Through meetings with staff and management, created several unique customer service training manuals to meet specific department needs.
Plan and conduct monthly training sessions to improve customer service skills of individual representatives; provide constant feedback on strengths and weaknesses.
*   Plan and oversee monthly feedback sessions with each department manager. These are designed to improve worker morale and production.

Director: Program Services   3/90-11/89
Utilized Lotus 1-2-3 to develop and administer the firm's Client Certification Exam.
Created a company reference module for all new employees.

Customer Service Representative   11/87-3/90
Acted as Operations Manager for four customer service divisions.
Responsible for troubleshooting with supervisors and claims managers from the nation's top 18 insurance companies.
*   Effectively hired, trained and monitored the performance of up to 12 Customer Service Representatives.
*   Managed budgets, payroll and bonus plans.

Customer Service Supervisor / Trainer   11/85-10/87
Gained hands-on experience in direct client relations and communications.

EDUCATION:
DePaul University of Nashville, Nashville, TN
Bachelor of Science Degree   6/84
Major: Psychology; Minor: Communications

The Wilhelm Franken Course, Nashville, TN
Courses included Dealing with Difficult People, Operations Management and How to be an Effective Supervisor.

LISA M. EARNEST   *COMBINATION/COLLEGE GRADUATE*

233 47th Street   518 College Avenue
Oak Lawn, IL 60457   Carbondale, IL 60115
708/555-3390: Permanent Address   Until May 1995: 815/555-3401

OBJECTIVE: A position where professional communication and organizational skills would be utilized and which offers the potential for career advancement.

PROFILE:
- Skilled in direct customer service, sales, writing and speech communications; experience in multimedia advertising, including ad design and the purchase of print and radio air time.

- Familiar with staff training and supervision; organize special events and conduct speeches and presentations in a professional manner.

- Experience in detailed research and report writing using WordStar, as well as data entry/retrieval on various databases.

EDUCATION: Southern Illinois University, Carbondale, IL
                           B.S. Degree   Graduated May, 1991
                           Major: Corporate Communications; Major GPA: 3.18/4.0

- As Executive Board Member of Alpha Sigma Alpha Sorority, acted as Foods Chairman and managed a $16,000 budget; supervised a cook and two waiters.
  As Assistant Social Chairman, planned numerous dances and social events.
- Assistant Advertising Representative, The Northern Star Newspaper. Communicated with customers and provided creative input on ad design. Reviewed ads via phone and ensured their prompt, accurate placement.
- Teaching Assistant for a course entitled Exceptional Persons in Society. Involved in stimulating group discussions, grading papers and testing.
- Teacher's Assistant for a Communications Class. Involved in program production and marketing.
- International Studies in Japan, Fall 1990. Completed several courses including East Asian Studies at Kansai Gaidai University, Hirakata City.
- Gained experience in Japanese language and culture.

EMPLOYMENT: Limited Express, Chicago Ridge, IL   Summers & Breaks, 1986-1991
                                 Sales Associate
                                 Handled direct customer service and sales, as well as merchandising and the set-up of retail displays.
                                 Maintained accurate inventories and consistently met sales goals.
                                 Involved in special promotions and the opening of two new stores, including occasional staff supervision.

- Earned the Gold Platter award for excellent client relations.

ANTHONY VARGAS

FUNCTIONAL

18 Windbrook Drive #101
Deer Grove, MA 10089

124/555-0372

OBJECTIVE:	***GENETIC ENGINEERING*** A position where diverse technical skills would be utilized.

EXPERIENCE:

- Experience in DNA cloning and subcloning using plasmid vectors; techniques include sterile handling of bacterial cultures, plasmid DNA purification and band separations by ultra centrifugation with CsCl gradient.

- Skilled in restriction enzyme splicing and separation of different size fragments on agarose gel electrophoresis, as well as DNA ligation and transformation into competent bacterial cells.

- Perform Sanger method DNA sequencing; experience in projects involving enzyme kinetics, protein purification/characterization and, quantitative/ qualitative chemistry.

- Analytical chemistry experience includes working with fat and carbohydrate substitutes; conduct viscosity analyses using modern viscometers.

- Determine particle sizes and counts; utilize Coulter multi-sizing instruments; familiar with titrations, microscopy and ion conductivity.

EMPLOYMENT:

NutraSweet, Deer Grove, MA   8/90-Present
Research Technologist - Subcontractor basis
Involved in projects related to the development of Simplesse and various carbohydrates.

EDUCATION:

Western Massachusetts University, Deer Grove, MA
M.A. Degree - Chemistry   1989-Present
Completed all courses toward Masters Degree in May, 1990. Currently completing a thesis entitled ``Genetic processing of T-DNA in agrobacteria.''

B.A. Degree - Chemistry   1986-1988
Emphasis in Biochemistry
Minor: Microbiology

Eglin Community College, Eglin, MA
Completed prerequisite courses.   1984-1986

Nursing School Graduate   1981
High School Graduate   1979

MATTHEW M. HAROLD   *COMBINATION*

5976 Spice Hill #5C
Method, MD 60090   108/555-1463

PROFILE:
- Extensive training and skills in Chemistry, including more than eight years of combined experience in laboratory procedures, product testing/inspection, quality control and customer relations.

- Familiar with system design and development; handle in-depth research and produce written and oral reports in a professional manner.

- Utilize Fortran, BASIC and MS Word for custom programs and correspondence writing.

EMPLOYMENT:
Toxic Removal Corporation, Arlington, ME

Summers, 1985-1989 and 1990-Present

Crew Member: Asbestos Abatement
Responsible for asbestos removal from commercial and residential buildings.
Train and supervise abatement crews in high-rise office buildings and residential structures.

Bartlett Manufacturing, Wheeling, ME   4/82-4/86
Assistant to the Production Supervisor
Tested wastewater chemistry and worked directly with management in water quality maintenance and improvement.
Responsible for the collection, storage and disposal of various hazardous wastes.

Quality Control Representative
Performed extensive laboratory testing of plating bath fluids.
Tested and maintained the quality of finished circuit boards.

Willis Widgets Corp. Batavia, ME   6/78-1/82
Quality Control / Customer Service Representative
Communicated with dealers and answered questions on part specifications
and use.
Maintained excellent quality of finished parts.

Astrolab, Batavia, ME   3/77-2/78
Technician
Assembled superconductor magnet systems as R&D Group Member.

Metals du Monde, Aurora, IL   2/76-11/76
Shipping / Material Handling Foreman

EDUCATION:
University of Tahoe, Lake Tahoe, NV   Graduated 12/89
B.S. Degree, Chemistry   Minor: Chemical Engineer
Courses involved the design of a distillation column, a separation process using heat transfer principles and a chemical separation plant.

Member of AICHE (1986-1988) and Delta Phi Fraternity.

MELISSA STARR *COMBINATION*

4568 Harvard Ocean Lane   Harvard, CO 12050   512/555-7297

OBJECTIVE: A position where talents in communications, business administration and human relations would be of value.

PROFILE:

♦ Plan and conduct written and oral presentations in a professional manner; proficient in training, lecturing and the development of teaching materials.

♦ Experience in sales, marketing and policy development; administer budgets and payroll; procure capital equipment and update/maintain inventories.

♦ Assist in the hiring, training and supervision of staff; experienced in personnel administration and the planning/implementation of special projects and events.

EMPLOYMENT: The Country Day School, Harvard, CO   1983-Present
Director
In charge of all operations at this preschool and kindergarten facility, including promotions, sales, marketing and budget coordination.
* Responsible for the set-up and maintenance of this growing business, including the hiring and supervision of all teaching staff.

Irish Grove School, Harvard, CO   1980-1983
Principal
Directed all aspects of management for 26 teachers, as well as the development of cost-effective policies and school procedures.
* Managed budgets and payroll as member of the Policy Committee Board.
* Developed and executed curricula for virtually all general subjects.
* Established student math, reading and psychological testing centers.

St. Peter Elementary School, Wauconda, IL   1971-1980
Principal
Supervised 22 teachers, including hiring, performance review and termination.
Created the science department and acquired all necessary capital equipment.
* Opened a new computer center, involving the cost-effective sourcing and purchasing of all computers and related peripherals.

Previous Experience:
More than ten years of experience teaching in various Catholic Schools. Taught grades 3 and 5 in general topics; taught Science and History at the Jr. High School level.

EDUCATION: Loyola University, Chicago, IL
M.Ed. Degree Emphasis: Administration and Supervision

Long Grove College, Chicago, IL
B.A. Degree Education

DANIEL D. SHARK   *COMBINATION*

120 Field Drive
Glenside, NY 10139   567/555-3729

PROFILE:

- Coordinate sales, marketing and distribution networks in worldwide markets; manage strategic planning and competitive analyses.

- Organize advertising, promotions and public relations activities; plan and conduct technical and sales presentations at meetings and trade shows with professional communication skills.

- Experience in hiring, training and supervising laboratory and technical staff, sales teams and operations management at virtually all levels of experience.

- Plan and implement budgets and long- & short-term business programs; handle comprehensive financial analysis, forecasting, modeling and spreadsheet development.

- Proven ability to convert profit losing operations to profit gainers through detailed planning and staff/management motivation.

- Executive-level talents in product development/introduction, international marketing and business administration, including full responsibility for P&L and new ventures.

**CAREER
BACKGROUND:**   <u>CDG Food Corporation,</u> Elmsford, CA   5/88-Present

Vice President / General Manager
In charge of U.S. business activities including primary responsibility for marketing and business development for this firm specializing in creating, distributing and marketing food ingredients worldwide; annual sales exceed $30 million.
Report directly to the president/owner and coordinate the cost-effective development of products including a natural MSG replacement, a line of amino acids and natural butyric acids and their related processes.

— Directly involved in hiring and training laboratory, administrative, accounting and research personnel.
— Responsible for five employees and all aspects of management for a professional sales and distribution network.
— Supervise a private labeling program for all products and processes which has increased international awareness of virtually all PTX endeavors.
— Increased baking industry market share for cultured whey products from 40 percent to 65 percent.
— Improved market awareness and exposure for PTX through regular involvement in a variety of trade advertising programs and conventions, including the Institute of Food Technology.

<u>Pennant Products, Inc.</u>, Rochester, NY   3/87-5/88
Currently a division of Van Den Bergh Foods Company.
Divisional Sales Manager
Personally directed marketing and sales functions for bakery products, mixes and frozen/prepared items in a 17-state region.
Hired, trained and supervised four territory managers and planned & implemented all marketing programs through interface with company president.

— Acquired and managed several national accounts.
— Developed and maintained all product distribution channels within the division.
— Established a national service relationship with such key accounts as Super Valu, Scribners, American Fruit, Nash Finch, Federated Foods and Sysco.
— Responsible for creating Pennant's first sales, distribution and service programs in Wisconsin, Minnesota, Iowa and Nebraska.

<u>New Zealand Milk Products/N.Z. Farms, Inc.</u>, Petaluma, CA   7/85-11/86
General Manager
Involved in the start-up and operation of this firm that packaged, marketed and sold specialty cheese products to retail accounts.
Hired and directed key managers for production, marketing, sales, advertising, retail promotion and general business administration.

— Created detailed short- and long-range business and marketing plans.
— Established a broker network and organized distribution of imported New Zealand cheeses throughout seven west-coast states.
— Successfully positioned New Zealand Milk Products firmly in profitable retail and food service markets.

<u>Quali-Tech, Inc.</u>, Chaska, MN   9/83-3/85
General Manager / National Sales Manager, Food Products Division
Developed all sales and marketing programs for this marketing and manufacturing group producing food ingredients.
Represented and marketed to industrial food manufacturers in the U.S. and Canada.

— NOTE: This division was formed following the purchase of the food ingredient division of the Peavey Company (listed below).
— As former Division Manager with Peavey, managed existing business and integrated totally new health food products and marketing programs.
— Introduced and marketed five new health foods and an industrial food ingredient.

EDUCATION: <u>University of Southern Minnesota</u>, Mankato, MN
                         B.S. Degree: Business Administration/Economics   Graduated 1968

TONY PROVENZANO   *COMBINATION*

750 Salem Drive #318
Hoffman Estates, IL 60194   708/555-2337

ENGINEERING / RESEARCH

EXPERIENCE:
- Comprehensive experience in digital signal processing and pattern recognition, as well as top-level research on neural networks.

- Extensive research, publications and/or experience in fuzzy logic, cybernetics, microprocessor-based controls and digital circuit design.

- Proficient in Fortran, BASIC and C; familiar with major software packages; conduct mathematical/system modeling and documentation.

- Skilled in Myoelectric Prosthesis and Biomedical signal processing, including EMG and EEG systems.

EMPLOYMENT:

<u>DDE: A unit of Super Signal,</u> Silicon Hill, IL   Contract Basis: 7/92-Present
Quality Control
Responsible for functional, cycle and production testing of computer-based turnstiles and systems in the QC department.
Located and solved numerous system bugs by producing various test environments.
* Diagnosed and corrected faults in system hardware.
* Assisted in the total redesign of a sensor board.

<u>Biomedical and Engineering Research Center,</u> Burgio, Sicily   2/90-6/92
Project Engineer
Defined and planned more than 50 research projects; involved in producing all related proposals and documentation.
Designed and adapted myoelectric prosthesis for clinical evaluation on humans.
Applied neural network approach for processing and classification of bioelectric signals including EEG, EP and EMG.
* As EEG Executive Supervisor, supervised 15 individuals including engineers, research staff and students.
* Set up an entire computer system for the center; configured PCs and produced customized data acquisition software.
* Developed a system to study and measure human performance with various hardware and software, including hand/eye tracking.

EDUCATION:

<u>Sicilian University of Technology,</u> Burgio, Sicily
M.S.E.E. Degree   Graduated 9/89
B.S.E.E. Degree   Graduated 2/87

PUBLICATIONS:
Researched and wrote more than 17 articles, including many on state-of-the-art subjects; complete list of articles available upon request.

CONTESSA M. BERGER   *COMBINATION*

2273 Seaview Blvd.
Peachtown, GA 21003   238/555-0160

OBJECTIVE: A Teaching position in Math or Science at the High School level.

PROFILE:
- ▸ Certified in grades 6-12, math and science, including experience in cooperative learning, lecturing, discussion and group management.

- ▸ Successful in teaching narrative, expository, descriptive and creative writing with an emphasis on style.

- ▸ Enjoy coaching cross-country and track; interested in leading student writing and reading clubs; plan and implement daily lessons using various study guides and audio/visual materials; utilize WordStar and Macintosh computers in the classroom.

TRAINING: **Student Teacher**   8/90-12/90
Atlanta High School, Atlanta, GA
Responsible for teaching two courses in American Literature, two courses in Regular English and a course in Basic English.
Taught sophomores, juniors and seniors; organized discussion groups and evaluated individual performance.
Topics included novels and short stories by authors such as Poe, Emerson, Thoreau, Cooper, Irving, Golding and Hawthorne.

* Taught English basics to a Polish immigrant, considered a zero English-speaking student.

EDUCATION: Southern Georgia University, Peachtown, GA   5/91
B.A. Degree
Major: English; Minor: History
* Dean's List, three semesters

PRIOR
EXPERIENCE: **Secretary,** Summer, 1987
Performed typing, telephone answering and general office work.
Employed in various waitress and retail positions throughout college.

PERSONAL: Willing to travel or relocate for the right opportunity.
Member of the Sierra Club and an active environmentalist.
Enjoy reading, jogging and regular exercise.

KATY J. COSENTINO

CHRONOLOGICAL with brief summaries

516 North West Avenue
Elmhurst, AK 30126

321/555-5154

GENERAL PSYCHOLOGY:

- Experience in assessment and therapy for groups, individuals, families, children and adolescents.

HUMAN RESOURCES:

- Extensive background in employee counseling and the development/documentation of plant safety and administrative programs.

EXPERIENCE:

M&M / SNICKERS, Elmhurst, AK   1974-Present

Special Projects Clerk, Technical Section   1986-Present
Responsibilities include editing and publishing the *Safety Newsletter* for all employees.
Design incentive programs to improve plant safety.
Process workers' compensation claims.
Maintain all records and financial reports related to special projects and arrange activities for associates.

- Member of Safety Promotions Committee.
- Serve on Management Safety Committee.

Special Projects Clerk, R & D Section   1985-1986
Directly involved in writing and producing a Good Manufacturing Practices Handbook, including the FDA's requirements for good manufacturing practices and organization standards. This is currently being distributed.
Assisted in installing a new chocolate plant in this facility.
Visited manufacturing plants in England and coordinated support for British employees visiting the Chicago plant. Arranged worker accommodations, as well as travelers' checks, access to charge cards and sightseeing.
Maintained cash receipts, financial records and clerical support.
Worked with up to 8 employees and helped relieve tension and stress related to various projects.

- Sampled products on a random basis to maintain quality to company standards.
- Conducted training programs for OSHA.
- Developed and presented a system to prepare employees for a major test.

Human Resources Representative   1974-1985
Conducted intervention counseling of employees with both medical and personal problems and referred them to appropriate doctors or other professionals as needed.
Communicated directly with employees regarding benefits, workers' compensation, accident/health benefits and long-term disability benefits.
Arranged activities for associates, including dances and dinners.
Screened applications, conducted interviews and recruited for various positions.

- Assisted in organizing a program for English as a second language.
- Explored options in developing an illiteracy program.
- Involved in counseling associates of lost family members.
- Assisted employees with alcohol-related problems in receiving necessary counseling and benefits.

EDUCATION:

Forest Institute, IL
Currently working toward **M.S. Degree** in Psychology
Expected graduation: September, 1991

National College of Education, Lombard, IL
M.A. Degree, Management and Human Resource Development, June 1985

Rosary College, River Forest, IL
B.A. Degree, Psychology, May 1982

Additional courses, 1986-Present:

- Theories of Personality
- Management of Addiction Treatment Programs
- Human Development 1 and Personal & Prof. Development 1
- Human Development 2 and Personal & Prof. Development 2

- Thinking, Motivation, Emotion and Personal & Prof. Development 3
- Sexual Abuse
- Biological Bases 1 and 3
- Biological Bases of Human Behavior 1 and 2: Perception and Maturation

- Psychopathology 3 and Psych. Intervention 3
- Clinical Skills 1
- Psychopathology and Psych. Assessment 1
- Psych Assessment 2 and Psych. Intervention 2
- Social Psychology and Psych. Assessment 3

- Research Design & Methods 1: Basic Statistics and Psych. Intervention 1
- Research Design & Methods 2: Advanced Stats. and Psychopathology 2
- Research Design & Methods 3: Advance Stats completed 6/19/90

ALBERT D. ANGLE   *COMBINATION/New Graduate*

Until May 20, 1995:   After May 20, 1995:
230 West Chase Avenue   2827 South Heatherton Lane
DeKalb, IL 60115   Streamwood, IL 60193
815/555-3166   708/555-1523

OBJECTIVE: A position utilizing skills and education in Mechanical Engineering and/or computer-aided product design.

PROFILE:
- Trained in mechanical engineering and AutoCad for product development; strong aptitude for learning new computer systems and technical procedures.

EDUCATION: <u>Northeastern Illinois University,</u> Charleston, IL
B.S. Degree: College of Engineering;   Expected Graduation: May, 1995
Major: Mechanical Engineerin; Minor: Mathematics
Major GPA: 3.04/4.0; Cumulative GPA: 3.00/4.00

* Courses included training in Statics, Dynamics and Fluids, as well as AutoCad and Thermodynamics/Heat Transfer systems.

<u>Judo Club,</u> Northeastern Illinois University, Charleston, IL   May, 1994-Present
Assistant Instructor / President
Train and supervise up to 23 students in two classes, including student motivation and performance evaluation.

<u>Continental Cablevision,</u> Palatine, IL   Summer, 1993
Intern
Assisted in producing special television programs.

EXPERIENCE: <u>Blackie's Plastic Mold Co.,</u> Addison, IL
Summer Internship   1991-1993
Responsible for the use and maintenance of lathes, mills, drill presses, grinders, band saws and various hand tools.
Involved in the production of steel and aluminum molds, including drilling and polishing of finished products.

<u>Gardner Tree and Landscaping,</u> Bensenville, IL
Supervisor   Summer, 1988
Managed up to seven employees in various landscaping activities.
Ensured customer satisfaction and maintained all equipment on a regular basis.

<u>Blue Suade Shoes,</u> Schaumburg, IL
Stock Clerk   1984-1985
Updated and maintained accurate inventories.
Handled shipping, receiving and pricing of merchandise.

ERICK B. STONE   *COMBINATION*

22167 Saw Towne Road   432/555-8807 Bus.
Red Villa, WI 40030   432/555-9040 Res.

DISTRIBUTION / WAREHOUSING

PROFILE:
- More than ten years in management and distribution activities, including full responsibility for warehouse organizing, employee supervision and system streamlining.

- Experience in freight routing, traffic management and cost-effective rate negotiation with freight carriers; assist in budget development and procedure planning/updating.

- Effectively train and motivate warehouse and support personnel at virtually all levels of experience.

- Work with senior-level staff in capital equipment purchasing and the set-up and maintenance of inventory control systems and computerized FI/FO operations.

CAREER BACKGROUND: J.B. Bachmann, Northern Distribution Center, Wheeling, WI   1981-Present
DISTRIBUTION SUPERVISOR   1984-Present
Manage all incoming and outgoing foreign and domestic shipments for this center, a division of the world's largest manufacturer and importer of gifts and specialty items.
Hire, train and supervise 20 employees in shipping/receiving and distribution procedures, including hiring, performance review and termination.
Purchase forklifts, conveyors, shelving and general office equipment.
Work directly with customs brokers; involved in cost-effective routing and trafficking on a daily basis.

* Through communications with management and programmers, established a computerized product locator system, requiring detailed zoning of the entire warehouse. Location and movement of all stock is tracked and updated by computer every four hours.
* Directly involved in the layout and organizing of three major warehouses, including the implementation of construction specifications with contractors.
* Created a safety lottery with cash incentives for all employees, resulting in a 65 percent decrease in reportable accident claims.
* Completed three seminars sponsored by Dakin, Inc. and presented by National Seminars, Inc. Topics included How to Supervise People, How to Handle Difficult People and How to Get Things Done.

Lead Position / Foreman   1982-1984
In charge of warehouse crews of up to 20 employees in order picking, truck loading/unloading and shipping.

Warehouse Crew Member   1981-1982

Erick B. Stone _____   **Page Two**

<u>The Sports House,</u> Bar & Restaurant, Ocean View, NE   1975-1981
Manager
Trained and supervised cooks, bartenders and wait staff in all restaurant procedures.
Utilized Excel to track payroll and other expenses.
Responsible for purchasing all food, beverages and entertainment for this high-volume
establishment.

* Maintained excellent quality of food and service.
* Involved in advertising, promotions and merchandising.

**PRIOR
EXPERIENCE:**   <u>Harrah's Casino,</u> Lake Tahoe, NV
Blackjack Dealer   1.5 Years

<u>The Pizza Palace,</u> Los Gatos, CA
Line Cook   8 Months

EDUCATION: <u>Willow Lake College,</u> Winona, MN   Graduated 1972
B.S. Degree   **Major: Political Science**
Major GPA: 3.1/4.0

<u>DePaul Academy,</u> Wilmette, IL
Graduate, College Preparatory School

BRUCE J. BARRET

COMBINATION

351 Mohawk Lane
Glenview, IL 60025

708/555-2705

PROFILE:

- More than 12 years of fixed income sales experience with a major firm, covering commercial banks, money managers and public pension funds.

- Extensive relationships within the Ohio and Western Pennsylvania banking communities.

- Comprehensive knowledge of products that include OTC options and swap-related activities.

EMPLOYMENT:

<u>Universal Partners, Inc.</u>, Chicago, IL
Vice President, Marketing   8/90-Present
Responsible for marketing money management services - for a registered investment advisor - to pension consultants, pension plan sponsors, corporations and high-net-worth individuals.

<u>Rodgers, Peabody & Company, Inc.</u>, Chicago, IL   4/78-8/90
Vice President, Fixed Income Sales   8/86-8/90
Covered a variety of institutional clients including major commercial banks, thrifts, public pension funds, money managers and state governments.
Geographic concentration of important relationships in Ohio and Western Pennsylvania.
Products included U.S. Governments, agencies, mortgages, CMO's, asset-backs, corporates, OTC options, swaps and futures.
Business included relative value sector swaps, yield curve arbitrage, option-related strategies and matched-funding transactions.

Vice President, Fixed Income Sales, Cleveland, OH   4/78-8/86
Marketed taxable, fixed income products to commercial banks, thrifts, insurance companies and state & local governments.
Supervised operations of a six-person institutional sales branch: 6/84-8/86.
Hired and trained staff; managed all aspects of sales and client servicing.
- Achieved shareholder status in 1982.
- Promoted from Vice President in 1980.

<u>Equibank, N.A.</u>, Pittsburgh, PA   6/76-4/78
Vice President, Manager: Taxable Trading Desk
Supervised operation of a seven-person trading desk, including hiring and training.
Coordinated training with the sales manager for optimum staff performance.

EDUCATION:

<u>Kent State University</u>, Kent, OH
M.B.A., Finance, 1973
B.B.A., Finance, 1970

JAMES C. COTS

COMBINATION

14 West Oakdale #2A
Chicago, IL 60657

312/555-8100 Ofc.
312/555-4014 Res.

EXPERIENCE:

- ▸ More than five years in retail leasing and commercial sales, including full responsibility for market research, competitive analysis and account acquisition/management.

- ▸ Handle strategic planning and sales forecasting; familiar with Lotus 1-2-3 and WordPerfect as well as NPV and IRR calculations.

- ▸ Developed or codeveloped 49,000 s.f. of retail and office space valued in excess of $6 million since 1988.

- ▸ Completed all courses toward CCIM Designation.

CAREER BACKGROUND:

Johnson Realty Group, Chicago, IL   1987-Present
Account Manager
Responsible for retail leasing and commercial property sales.
Act as leasing agent for retail property owners.
Proven ability to develop profitable relationships with major clientele.
- Completed 30 deals ranging from 1,000 to 15,000 s.f. in 1990.
- Cumulative dollar volume of deals in excess of $10 million, 1989-present.
- Sales of commercial and retail properties have exceeded $3 million per year since 1987.

Plotkin & Company, Chicago, IL   1985-1987
Broker
Directly involved in the opening of this company.
Worked extensively with national retailers including K-Mart.

Acted as lead broker for:
- Riverplace shopping center, 80,000 s.f., in Lansing, IL.
- Plaza Del Prado shopping center, 125,000 s.f., Glenview, IL.
- Oak Creek Plaza shopping center, 360,000 s.f., Mundelein, IL.

Wasilov & Zifkin Distributors, Philadelphia, PA   1980-1985
President / Owner
Successfully imported, distributed and serviced high-end restaurant equipment.
- Sales grew from $30,000 to $400,000 in the first four years.
- This business was sold in 1985 at a substantial profit.

EDUCATION:

Michigan State University, East Lansing, MI
B.A. Degree, Geography   1975

University of Michigan, Ann Arbor, MI
Teaching Certificate   1976

DOUGLAS T. KLATT

COMBINATION

4584 Riverview Circle
Wetville, IL 60070
708/555-8229

OBJECTIVE: A position in retail operations or management, where profit-building skills and self-motivation would be utilized.

PROFILE:
- Successful experience in retail management, including four years in multiunit supervision with total P&L responsibility.

- Coordinate bookkeeping, loss prevention, inventory control and financial statement preparation using Lotus and Excel on DOS systems.

- Hire, train and motivate store personnel in sales and professional customer service; proven ability to reduce staff turnover with personal communication skills.

EXPERIENCE: SUPERTRON VIDEO WAREHOUSE, Dundee, IL   12/81-Present
Store / District Manager
Oversee all procedures and operations at three video stores, in a chain of 21.
Train and supervise up to 25 employees in customer relations, store decorating and the design of creative window displays.
Plan and implement special in-store promotions and merchandising strategies.
Determine store layouts and best uses of P.O.P. displays.
Responsible for general ledger and journal updating, as well as accounting activities at all three stores.

- * Utilize a menu-driven computer system.
- * Work directly with suppliers and contractors on a daily basis.
- * Currently manage this chain's #1 store.
- * Maintain high worker morale and dedication.

EDUCATION: Central Michigan College, St. Joseph, MI   1980-1981
- * Overall GPA: 3.8/4.0

Successful completion of classes in:
- * Management
- * Business Law
- * Economics
- * Accounting

Randall High School, Randall, MI
Graduate   1980

BELINDA M. ELSON　　　　　*COMBINATION/VETERAN*

127 Kings Drive East　　　　　　　　　　　　　　　　312/555-2747 Ofc.
Addison, IL 60101　　　　　　　　　　　　　　　　　708/555-3461 Res.

ENGINEERING / TECHNICAL SUPPORT

EXPERIENCE:

♦ More than seven years in computer and communication system repair and maintenance, including full responsibility for technical service and support.

♦ Repair and troubleshoot digital, voice, data and secure communications; interface with SAT COM, HF and Wideband systems.

♦ Experience in system analysis, teardown, repair and documentation; skilled in a full range of specialty tools, mock-ups and test equipment for preventive maintenance.

♦ Assist in system/site layouts, inventory control and technical staff training & supervision.

♦ Skilled in WordPerfect, WordStar, Lotus 1-2-3, Harvard Graphics and FormTool.

EMPLOYMENT:　　Air National Guard, O'Hare Field, Chicago, IL　　Full-time: 1988-Present
　　　　　　　　　　　　　　　　　　　　　　　　　　　　and Weekends, 1985-Present
Digital Electronics Technician　　　　　　　　　　　　　　10/88-Present
Various duties include:

Engineering, 20%:
Responsible for the prompt repair and maintenance of control systems and digital voice, data and secure communication devices.
Plan and implement communication system maintenance functions.
Manage full squadron site layouts, including cable runs in excess of 20,000 feet and instrumentation/cross-connects for up to 700 items.
* Oversee programming of 600-line switchboards, including proper interfacing and channel assignments.
* Update and maintain system inventories for deployment; interface with SAT COM, HF and Wideband systems.

Maintenance, 30%:
Conduct preventive maintenance inspections and scheduled/unscheduled troubleshooting of six systems and equipment; utilize special tools, fixtures and test equipment.

Workcenter Management Duties, 20%:
Respond to priority maintenance requirements and establish/maintain bench stocks; manage an equipment account valued up to $14 million; maintain a repair cycle and an ongoing corrosion control programs.

Training, 15%:
Established Work Center training programs for five communication systems, including three different AFSCs (AF SP Cds).
Effectively train and supervise 20 personnel; conduct classes for both operations and maintenance; organize and develop training aids, including reference guides.

Documentation, 10%:
Document maintenance actions and manage a T.O. file of 150 manuals.

Safety, 5%:
Safely maintain all work areas and facilities.

Secretary / Typing   1/88-9/88
Handled a full range of secretarial functions, including word processing, general reception, posting of regulations and distribution of computer products to more than six sections and 13 units.
Expedited telephone calls and correspondence in a professional manner.

First Western Mortgage Company/Banner Services, Palatine, IL
Receptionist / Personnel Clerk   6/86-8/87
Scheduled appointments, answered telephones and typed/distributed correspondence for staff and management.
Reformatted and organized all personnel files; typed letters and forms while controlling the flow of incoming resumes.
Processed outgoing mail and updated files; screened telephone calls and supervised one temporary employee in a professional manner.

Air National Guard, part-time
Electronic Computer & Switching Systems Specialist   7/85-5/86
Gained hands-on experience with electronic principles, including integrated and transistor circuits, pulsing techniques, shift registers, counters, buffers, logic gates and flip flops.
* Trained in binary, octal and hexidecimal numbering systems, basic computer programming and the writing of diagnostic test routines for locating failures.
* Interpreted orders, schematics and wiring diagrams.

EDUCATION: Illinois State University, Normal, IL   1988-1989
Liberal arts courses included English, Psychology, Economics and Mathematics.

Wright Junior College, Chicago, IL   1986-1987
Classes included Writing and Drama

Community College of the Air Force   1985-1986
Completed courses in Electronics

GARY D. BUSSMAN

COMBINATION

3121 Land Street
Mundelein, IL 60060

708/555-0553

PRODUCT DEVELOPMENT / MARKETING

PROFILE:

♦ Comprehensive experience in creative product development, including full responsibility for design, marketing and licensing with major international firms.

♦ Experience in the setup and management of a very successful, multimillion dollar company; coordinate budgets, procedures and staffing.

♦ Plan and conduct top-level sales presentations and negotiate contracts for materials and worldwide distribution in the gift/social expression industry.

♦ Design and implement customized retail programs and displays, as well as coordinated product lines.

♦ Strong knowledge of major international suppliers, producers and markets; traveled extensively throughout Hong Kong, Japan, Taiwan, Korea and China; oversee trade show presentations worldwide.

EMPLOYMENT: R.A.S. Industries, Barrington, IL   10/82-1/95

CREATIVE DIRECTOR
Fully responsible for initiating this company's most successful product line, currently its sole product. This is now the world's largest manufacturer of metalized (Mylar) balloons for the social expression industry.
Directed highly successful licensing programs and negotiations with such companies as Hallmark Cards, American Greetings, Miller Brewing and Anheuser Busch; worked closely with licensors for Jurassic Park, Snoopy, Garfield and Hanna Barbera characters.
Handled all development for highly successful product lines from initial concept to completion.
Hired and supervised a creative staff of five artists, a product development coordinator and a print production coordinator; organized all work through freelance artists.

▸ Expanded sales from $2 million in 1982 to $31 million in 1994.
▸ Personally responsible for acquiring and managing hundreds of accounts, including those listed above.
▸ Coordinated all product development and art design needs for the European Subsidiary.

- ► Developed a very profitable custom products division.
- ► Implemented a complete, state-of-the-art computer design system to produce original mugs, gift bags, candy products and plush toys.
- ► Handled extensive international sales and directed the design and layout of exhibits at national and international trade shows.
- ► Worked closely with attorneys and legal staff regarding patent and copyright matters related to company designs and ideas.
- ► Established all contacts and vendors in the Orient; directed international sales to territories not reached by the European subsidiary.
- ► Initiated a dynamic, in-store display program, used by retail and national chain stores.

<u>Arthur Fulmer Company,</u> Memphis, TN   11/80-10/82
SALES REPRESENTATIVE
Performed sales of motorcycle and car accessories to hundreds of dealerships and parts houses throughout Michigan.
Products included radios, helmets and seat covers.
Gained an excellent background in dealership operations.

- ► Earned special award as Salesman of the Year.

<u>Unique Concepts/Silver Sails,</u> Grand Rapids, MI   9/77-10/80
OWNER / DISTRIBUTOR
Responsible for the setup and operation of this company, the first worldwide sales and marketing firm for a unique new product, currently sold at more than 50,000 locations.

<u>Credit Thrift Company,</u> Grand Rapids, MI   1974-1977
COLLECTOR / MANAGEMENT TRAINEE

<u>Garr's Honda,</u> Grand Rapids, MI   Summers, 1968-1973 and 1974-1977
MOTORCYCLE SALES REPRESENTATIVE
Gained comprehensive experience in motorcycle lines, accessories and dealership activities, with direct sales to a wide range of customers.

EDUCATION: <u>Ferris State University,</u> Big Rapids, MI   Graduated 1973
B.S. Degree: Business Administration

PAUL LENNON   *COMBINATION*

32114 Caster Court
Streamwood, IL 60107   708/555-1638

PROJECT ENGINEERING / SUPERVISION

PROFILE:

♦ More than 12 years in virtually all aspects of project engineering, machine design/building and secondary tooling, including full management responsibilities.

♦ Skilled in equipment design & fabrication from concept to completion; experience with Pneumatic & Hydraulic systems & components, automation equipment, Mechanical & Electrical systems and a full range of custom and specialty products.

♦ Utilize tracer lathes and a wide range of mills, drilling/tapping machines and shop equipment; proficient in spin tooling and secondary die making.

♦ Handle cost-effective purchasing of parts and materials; skilled in vendor relations; handle price quoting, sales presentations and proposal writing.

♦ Plan and implement budgets; perform job/labor estimates; oversee quality control and hire, train & supervise shop staff and management.

♦ Proficient in EASY CAD and CAD KEY; familiar with AutoCad and Lotus 1-2-3; skilled machinist, tool & die maker and welder: MIG and ARC.

EMPLOYMENT: <u>SuperFast Tool & Machine,</u> Dearborn, IL   1981-Present
General Manager   1986-Present
Responsible for virtually all shop operations including the design, troubleshooting and assembly of automated equipment, including drilling, milling and tapping machines.
In charge of quality control, purchasing of state-of-the-art equipment, professional customer relations and service at all levels.
Duties include extensive design work, programming of controllers, general/hard wiring of relay logic circuits and panel wiring.
Oversee worker hiring and training; assist in supervising all departments.
Perform detailed job estimating and price quoting.
Maintain excellent quality control to strict tolerances; develop & maintain excellent customer satisfaction and referral business.
Accounts include a major lighting manufacturer; analyze equipment/material needs and produce custom products on an as-needed basis.

→ Personally responsible for sales of up to $300,000 annually.
→ Performed field assembly and repair for a 12,000-lb. rotary press.
→ Directed the sale of this company in February of 1992.

Shop Manager   1983-1986
Primarily responsible for all machine shop operations including the design, manufacturing and assembly of secondary tooling and small automated equipment. Installed and programmed controllers.
Hired, trained and supervised up to five machinists; conducted performance appraisals and disciplinary actions as needed.
Developed manufacturing systems and custom, automated drilling and tapping equipment, as well as small electrical and pneumatic devices for both large and small accounts.

→   Sold/expedited up to $200,000 in new business annually.
→   Maintained excellent customer relations and developed a strong base of customer referrals.

Machinist/Assembler   1981-1983
Gained experience in virtually all machine shop operations and equipment: vertical/horizontal mills, lathes, grinders and various welders.
Assembled equipment and handled troubleshooting, blueprint reading/interpretation and customer relations as needed.

EDUCATION: Parker Hannifin Corporation, North Aurora, IL
                        Certificate
                        Industrial Power Training   1992

                        Allen-Bradley Corporation, Chicago, IL
                        Certificates:
                        Customer Support Services and Programmable Controllers   1984

                        Elgin Community College, Elgin, IL
                        Center for Employee and Management Development
                        Certificates:
                        Advanced Diemaking   Third-Year Level 1984
                        Basic Diemaking   1983

                        →   Completed courses in Lotus 1-2-3, CAD/CAM, DOS, Metallurgy and College Algebra.

                        Davea Center, Addison, IL
                        Certificate:
                        Machine Tool Operation   1980-1981

                        College of DuPage, Glen Ellyn, IL   1981
                        Classes included Advanced Machine Shop Operations, Manufacturing Technology, Welding Technology and Machine Shop Technology.

BETH STARR

(Current)	*COMBINATION*
3245 Acorn Court	(Temporary)
Wheeling, IL 60090 708/555-9651	8350 Greensboro Drive
	McLean, VA 22101 432/555-2828

SKILLS & EXPERIENCE:

Human Resources Management / Training & Development

◆ Proven ability to develop innovative programs and policies for compensation, training/development, recruitment and performance management.

◆ Design and conduct training programs at all corporate levels to promote major change initiatives; train/coordinate teams in total quality management.

◆ Negotiate union and non-union labor contracts; resolve complex grievances and employee relations issues; manage the integration of new manufacturing processes.

◆ Perform corporate/government relations and lobbying; conduct key presentations and interface with government officials and industry leaders as a corporate liaison.

EDUCATION:

<u>Cornell University,</u> Ithaca, NY   1989
Masters of Industrial and Labor Relations
Granted full Teaching/Research Assistantship. GPA: 3.7/4.0

<u>University of Cincinnati,</u> Cincinnati, OH   1987
Bachelor of Arts: Personnel Management/Industrial Relations
Granted Academic Scholarship by ASPA. Phi Beta Kappa and Mortar Board;
McMicken Honors College. GPA: 3.9/4.0

EMPLOYMENT:

<u>Transunion, Inc.,</u> Washington, D.C. Area   1989-1995
Human Resources Manager, Command Support Division   1991-1995
Manage all human resource functions for more than 400 technical and professional employees, including daily oversight of employee relations, policy application, salary administration and staffing.
Compensation Manager for the entire division, responsible for compensation/recognition strategies and award programs.
• Introduced the concept of variable compensation for higher performance and ensured its integration into current business strategies.
• Developed and conducted training programs to support performance management and quality initiatives.

Management Associate, Corporate Headquarters   1989-1991
Chosen to participate in a two-year, fast-track management development program, geared to provide company-wide experience and perspective in various sectors. Rotational assignments included:

Corporate Staff:
Planned and coordinated college relations programs.
- Screened and recruited staff and management.

Automotive Sector:
Participated in union contract negotiations involving hundreds of workers at a major automotive components plant.
- Facilitated the first successful workcell program and coordinated all cross-training efforts.
- Consolidated 250 job codes into ten and implemented a JIT work system, which greatly reduced waste and labor costs.

Government Relations:
Performed analyses of all public policy issues related to the air bag industry and presented a white paper on findings. Conducted key speeches, presentations & lobbying for government officials and industry executives to win the endorsement of airbag legislation.

Space and Defense:
Developed and implemented a training program for expatriates.

<u>Wheat Management Consultants,</u> New York, NY   Summer, 1988
Summer Associate
Analyzed the content of positions and wrote job descriptions, applying a point factor system to develop pay practices and strategies for clients.
- Assisted a Japanese trading firm in creating a performance appraisal system that integrated Japanese approaches with American practices.
- Conducted a communications audit and culture assessment for a manufacturing firm in rapid growth.

<u>Humana Incorporated,</u> Hopital de la Tour, Geneva, Switzerland   Summer, 1987
International Human Resources Representative
Developed a hospital-wide employee training program in guest relations and customer service.
- Assisted the executive director with the introduction/implementation of a Management-by-Objectives evaluation system.
- Conducted business matters in French.

<u>General Electric, Aircraft Division,</u> Cincinnati, OH   1986
Intern: Employee Relations Department
Researched/wrote a proposal for the plant's first technical training program.
- Involved in the design and implementation of a Multi-Skilled Job Reclassification Project to consolidate job codes and develop multiplicity of skills among hourly workers and shift operations - from a line to a workcell team process.

LEONARD A. CIRCUIT

COMBINATION

231 Blue Glen Lane
Glendale Heights, IL 60139

708/555-3118

PRODUCT DESIGN / DEVELOPMENT

PROFILE:

▸ More than ten years in drafting and CAD systems, including product research, design, development and testing.

▸ Utilize Windows and AS400 for customizing CAD applications; skilled in Rasterex, Automanager and Teradyne on System 38s and PCs.

▸ Handle sourcing and purchasing of parts and components, as well as inventory control, production scheduling, project tracking/documentation and technical staff training.

EMPLOYMENT:

Evanston/Rogers Corporation, Addison, IL   4/85-Present
Mechanical / Electrical Draftsman
Perform all aspects of product design and development from blueprints, requiring constant communications with electrical/mechanical engineers, production supervisors and customers.
Design, update and troubleshoot prototypes for sheet metal and electrical control panels, used primarily in industrial and commercial refrigeration units.
Provide instructions for brazing, soldering and welding; materials include steel & copper tubing, steel and aluminum.
Interpret blueprints for wiring to customer specs; utilize ohm meters and ensure accuracy and feasibility of all wiring and related systems.
→ Directly involved in production line setup and streamlining.
→ Major accounts include Hussman, Baxter, the Shedd Aquarium and major supermarket chains.

Electrical Assembler / Department Supervisor   4/85-4/88
Established production schedules and performed wiring, assembly and testing of electrical control panels.
Coordinated stock levels to correspond with demand, resulting in a major savings.
Trained and supervised five employees in procedures and operations.

Rockwell International, Downers Grove, IL   9/79-3/85
Electrical Repair / Troubleshooter
Operated a Teradyne system and OHM meter
Responsible for electrical troubleshooting and repair of telecommunication systems, including wiring and soldering backplates.

EDUCATION:

MIMA: Midwest Industrial Management Association, Westchester, IL
Completed training in Supervision, Supervision Psychology and Basic Electricity.

Hussman Institute, Bridgeton, MO
Trained in various state-of-the-art engineering applications.

Resume Index by Profession